EVOLVE
OR DIE

EVOLVE
OR DIE

SEVEN STEPS TO
RETHINK
THE WAY YOU DO
BUSINESS

ROBIN CROW

WILEY

John Wiley & Sons, Inc.

Published by John Wiley & Sons, Inc., Hoboken, New Jersey.
Published simultaneously in Canada.

For general information on our other products and services or for technical support, please contact our Customer Care Department within the United States at (800) 762-2974, outside the United States at (317) 572-3993 or fax (317) 572-4002.

Wiley also publishes its books in a variety of electronic formats. Some content that appears in print may not be available in electronic books. For more information about Wiley products, visit our web site at www.wiley.com.

Library of Congress Cataloging-in-Publication Data:

Crow, Robin, 1953–
    Evolve or die : seven steps to rethink the way you do business / Robin Crow.
       p. cm.
    ISBN 978-0-470-59345-5 (cloth)
    1. Organizational change.   2. Management.   I. Title.
    HD58.8.C764 2010
    658.4'06–dc22

                                         2009050973

Printed in the United States of America.

10   9   8   7   6   5   4   3

This book is dedicated to my four children...Savannah, Nakota, Joseph, and Andrew. Your love has inspired the writing of this book, and your future has made it necessary.

Contents

Acknowledgments

Evolve or Die came into existence only with the help of some truly remarkable, innovative, and talented people, all of which I am forever grateful to have on my team. It is with deep appreciation that I would like to thank Henry James, Jeff Jacob, Shelley Bright, Tim Bays, and Stephanie Capps for lending your insight, expertise, and debate in bringing this book reference to life.

A special thanks to . . .

The great team at John Wiley & Sons . . . Matt Holt, Lauren Lynch, Christine Moore, Linda Indig, and James Bennett.

My staff and support teams: Jeff Jacob, Matt Crum, Dave Hagen, Shelly Sharer, Mike Carr, Tim Coyle, Colin Heldt, Stephanie Capps, Melissa Fuller, and Dennis Anderson.

Crow Company Interns . . . Janee' Proffitt, Whitney Hoffman, Libby Reinhart, Chantal Lotane, and Lindsey Donovan.

Dark Horse Recoding interns . . . Ryan Goldbacher, Joshua Moss, Dustin Martin, Chris Yeager, Matt Hamilton, Taylor Reynaga, Ryan Sweeten, Alex Michalski, Brandon McGraw, Nick Kallstrom, Adam Latz, Chris Owens, Jeremiah

Shaver, Colby Smith, Patrick Fallon, Brendan Morris, Tom Shaver, Joe Ferguson, Peter Harris, Evan Shields, and Shane Stever.

An extra special thanks to ...

Chris Martenson, whose insights on converging global issues were a wake-up call for me and inspired this work.

About the Author

Robin Crow has forged a remarkable career on his journey from struggling musician to national recording artist, and then on to his startling success as entrepreneur and business owner. His company, Dark Horse Recording, a four-studio complex he built from the ground up, has set the gold standard for customer service and excellence in the recording industry, and is home to Faith Hill, Ashley Judd, Neil Diamond, Taylor Swift, Tim McGraw, Michael W. Smith, Jewel, and Alison Krauss to name a few. As a speaker, performer, and author he has appeared on countless television programs, released 9 albums, and has presented at more than 2,100 events.

Crow lectures widely on the implications of global issues and their effects on business sustainability. His other books include *The Power of an Idea, Rock Solid Leadership,* and *Jump and the Net will appear.* Robin lives in Franklin, Tennessee, and serves on the boards of several philanthropic organizations. He loves hanging out with his four children, throwing large barbecues for his studio clients and friends, and spending as much time as possible in the Rocky Mountains.

Introduction

It was a crisp, cool Saturday morning in April 2008. Gas prices were hovering at $4 a gallon, the great housing bubble had finally started to burst, and the nation was bracing for the worst economic disaster since the Great Depression. Other than that, it was just another typical day in Nashville.

My plan was simple: to swing by the local bookstore to pick up a couple magazines to research a book I was writing, and return home. As I was walking out of the house, I asked Savannah (my then-12-year-old daughter) if she wanted to join me. Fifteen minutes later we were pulling into an enormous parking lot, surrounded by outlet stores and restaurants that stretched for several blocks. Savannah turned to me and said, "Hey Dad, there's a Starbucks. Would you drop me off so I can pick up a hot chocolate, then I'll come find you at the store? And oh yeah, can I have $4?" Somewhere I heard it was a rule that dads are supposed to spoil their daughters, so I smiled and said, "Of course."

As I pulled closer to the Starbucks entrance, I was stunned by what I saw. At least a dozen cars were lined up at the drive-through with motors running, and all but one were expansive SUVs. And for what . . . a cup of coffee? Didn't anyone get the memo? Remember the energy crunch . . . plunging real-estate values . . . the economic crisis . . . global warming? Any one of these threats is reason enough to rethink being so wasteful. But there wasn't a care in the world among these well-intentioned Nashvillians kicking off their weekend in style. What could possibly be wrong?

Perhaps I was observing a microcosm of an overindulgent, bloated, and shortsighted America. But this was a neighborhood of family-oriented, community-minded, well-educated, and financially successful people; what were they thinking? Have we become so lazy that we can't even get out of our cars for a cup of coffee? And isn't this the kind of mentality that led to the economic crash in the first place? Apparently, $4 for a gallon of gas was still not enough to dissuade us from driving to get a latte or to turning off our engines—which only makes me wonder what it *will* take for us to get the message.

Knowing is not enough; we must apply!

—Goethe

You cannot be an effective leader in the twenty-first century without acknowledging that we are facing challenges of an unprecedented size and scope. World poverty, terrorism, a bankrupt economy, the energy crunch, and climate change are just a few of the countless and complex issues that we encounter every single day. And all of it is having a profound effect on your company; right here, right now. Business growth cannot be sustained if it remains in its present form. In fact, we can already see the early stages of the disintegration of traditional business models. Many of the excesses of the 1990s and early 2000s are by now proving fatal to the business leaders who've been focused on the past instead of the future. Just look at automobile giant

GM's fourth-largest U.S. bankruptcy on record. In an effort to restructure his failing company, CEO Fritz Henderson requested a government bailout and made the statement that "business as usual is over." But business as usual should have been over 20 years ago! Other companies like GM—who continue to run their businesses without acknowledging events *as they occur*—are in for big trouble. We must become business leaders who look well into the future and create our plans and projections based on thinking beyond one or two quarters ahead.

Going forward, creating more efficient business systems will become the holy grail of professional success. After the crash of 2008, it's a whole new ball game. The greatest fortunes of the next decade will likely come from entrepreneurs and business leaders who will find innovative, efficient, and valuable ways to deliver new products and services. That will probably mean less SUVs and fewer $4 cups of coffee.

All you have to do is begin stacking the exponential graphs of diminishing resources like coal, fish, and forest against the graphs of expanding population, our accelerating need for more oil, more food, and every other gift of nature—and the truth becomes clear. The party is over. The time for greed is over. The time for empty speeches, excuses, and half measures is over.

Although many of these problems seem bigger than any of the solutions that have been proposed for them, I'm going to prove to you beyond a shadow of a doubt in the pages of this book how achieving business sustainability and saving the planet—which in turn will save our businesses—tie neatly together with one common thread. I'm going to lay out principles that can be put to use by entrepreneurs and businesses of all sizes to experience better, faster results with consistent profitability.

Success means we go to sleep at night knowing that our talents and
abilities were used in a way that served others.

—Marianne Williamson

Do you remember those disaster movies in which a comet is headed toward earth? In an effort to survive the impending doom, people from all parts of the globe begin working together to find a solution, and realize in the process that all of their supposed differences aren't so important after all. All that matters is their willingness to unite forces and to do whatever it takes to somehow solve the problem—because if they don't, they know they're doomed—all of them.

There's a parallel here to our own world, as banks, automobile companies, and other institutions on which we used to depend are becoming increasingly unstable and slowly crumbling. American jobs are being outsourced to China and India. Now we find ourselves engaged in a struggle against terrorism, as well as wars in Iraq and Afghanistan. We're dealing with environmental issues that threaten our existence. And like it or not, these changes will continue to accelerate. The economic crash of 2008 has ushered in a new era where most businesses are going to have to evolve or die—not unlike the premise of those disaster movies.

He who refuses to embrace a unique opportunity loses the prize as
surely as if he had tried and failed.

—William James

These are times that try men's souls. It may seem that the world is spinning out of control as everything continues to change at a dizzying pace; but one thing that hasn't changed is the power and resilience of the human spirit. Rethinking your organization won't just profoundly affect your bottom line, it will enhance the world around us as well. Changing business for the better will change the world for the better. I believe—admittedly, somewhat optimistically—that we have the capacity to set aside our petty distractions and rise to the challenge that history is presenting us.

Evolve or Die is about creating better ways to move business forward; and in order for that to happen, we must move forward personally—as individuals—as well. It's time to stop viewing life solely through the lens of immediate self-interest and crass materialism, and expand our vision about what is possible. We must develop a culture of shared sacrifice—and that starts with personal leadership. We will have to forfeit to some degree in the short term for greater rewards down the line; we must make concessions so that our children will be able to enjoy the same life that we grew up taking for granted.

Russian novelist Leo Tolstoy once said, "Before we can change our world, we must first change ourselves." In many ways, his quote represents the underlying theme of this book. Yes, it's about business growth, but it's also about making ourselves better today than we were yesterday. It's about overcoming apathy and changing the way we look at the world—thereby changing the way we approach business as well. Then there will be no limits to what we can achieve.

EVOLVE
ᴼᴿDIE

PART I

Something Has to Give

1

Who Are You Listening To?

The Circus Is Coming to Town

On June 26, 2007, two Ethiopian soldiers were killed and two wounded in a roadside bombing in Mogadishu. On that same day, the Energy Department announced that it was creating three bio-energy research centers in an effort to find new ways to turn green plants into fuel.

But if you had been watching TV that day—no matter what channel you turned to—you would have found Paris Hilton to be the main event. Was she the sole survivor of an airplane crash? Had she discovered a cure for cancer? Did she donate a million dollars to start a homeless shelter? Not by a long shot. Hilton had been released from jail after serving a 20-day sentence for violating her probation in a drunken driving case. Waiting outside of L.A.'s Century Regional Detention Facility was a crush of *paparazzi* giving her the kind of attention you might expect for the President or the Pope; indeed, a full-fledged media circus.

It's All About the Ratings

Why do CNN and Fox News broadcast absurd events like Hilton's antics? In a word: *ratings*. These media outlets know that drama sells, and therefore decide what to air based not on real relevance or genuine importance, but on what will keep viewers tuned in and turned on. If you have a big mouth, strong opinions, and a flair for the dramatic, you just might have a career in television; just ask Ann Coulter, Rush Limbaugh, Keith Olbermann, or Bill Maher. Though I'm often amazed that people take them seriously, you've got to give them credit: they know that the louder they shout—the more argumentative, over-the-top, and controversial they are—the higher their books will climb on the bestseller lists, and the more viewers they'll grab. The "news" we get from watching television, mass-market books, or the Internet is compromised because the bottom line is that every news program lives or dies by ratings, and drama—trivial though it may be—drives ratings.

The Approaching Perfect Storm

Back in the real world, however, there is a convergence of truly threatening issues—that *will* affect your business, family, and quality of life—and that convergence is building momentum. Accelerating population, diminishing natural resources, increasing demand for energy, and our teetering environment are all ticking time bombs, even if they are not yet dramatic enough to merit primetime news coverage.

All four of these *real* issues will have far-reaching implications for the way you conduct business going forward. These are not conspiracies or best-kept secrets; all are the subject of countless books, magazine articles, and documentaries. Put them all together, and you have a *perfect storm* that cannot be ignored; yet that's exactly what the mainstream media (and our society) seems to be doing. We're like an ostrich that puts its head in the sand when danger is approaching; not too smart for the ostrich, or your business, either.

Living in a Bubble

Just last week I got a haircut from a delightful young woman whom I had never met before. She seemed bright, friendly, outgoing, and inquisitive, asking me one question after another. Once I told her that I was an author, she responded by asking, "What kind of books do you write?" I began telling her about a book I was currently writing (the one you are reading now), which delves into several critical issues that we are all going to have to face—particularly in business. I then inquired whether any of these challenges were of concern to her, and her response was, "No, I just live in my own little bubble and hope that everything will be okay." I realized her sentiments likely represent the views of most "average" Americans—happy to remain unaware and blissfully ignorant of severe and impending situations until they are personally affected. Well, that time is now, whether they know it or not.

Taking into consideration the many current global issues, savvy business leaders are starting to recognize that in order to succeed in the twenty-first century, we have no choice but to evolve or die.

Whether we choose to acknowledge it, we live and work together on a small planet that's interconnected in many complex
ways—many of which even experts don't fully understand. We
are at the beginning phases of an unprecedented turning point
in all of human history with the convergence of four global
issues—all taking place simultaneously. These issues—which I
list and briefly explain below—will most certainly impact your
business and therefore deserve your fullest attention. Your understanding of how to adapt your business to these four challenges
will be crucial to your company and your career's success, and
will determine which opportunities lie ahead.

1. Overpopulation
2. Diminishing natural resources
3. Global need for more energy
4. Environmental damage

*The best time to plant a tree is 20 years ago. The second best time
to plant a tree is today.*
                                                    —African Proverb

Overpopulation

Overpopulation is an incredibly dire yet oft-ignored issue. The
problem is not just the number of people on the planet, but
their "per-capita impact" on the environment each person has—
particularly in highly developed countries like the United States.
Citizens in developed nations consume 32 times more resources
and create 32 times more waste than those living in third-world
countries.

There were only 3 billion people living on this planet in 1959. By 1999—40 years later—the population had *doubled* to 6 billion. Most population experts agree that by 2040, there will be some *9 billion people* all sharing the same limited air, water, energy, and other natural resources. (See Figure 1.1) Though the planet hasn't gotten any bigger or richer in resources in the past half century, it has gotten exponentially more populated. There is no one who will *not* be affected by this; you and your business will be operating in an overcrowded world and will have to cope with growing populations that will need clean air, clean water, food, jobs, housing, and health care.

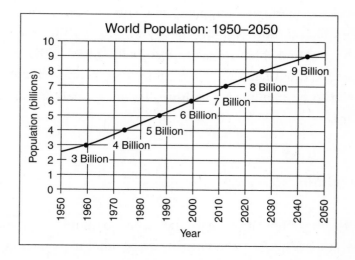

Figure 1.1 **POPULATION GROWTH CONTINUES.** **As the earth's population continues to climb, our natural resources on which every business depends are diminishing. As we squeeze in the next 3 billion people, only those businesses that are highly efficient and highly evolved will survive.**
Source: **U.S. Census Bureau, International Data Base, June 2009 update (www.census.gov/ipc/www/idb/worldpopgraph.php).**

In 1968, Paul Ehrlich's best-selling book *The Population Bomb* warned us of what would happen if the world population kept growing at the same pace. The book was a popular item for discussion on the cocktail party circuit back in the 1960s, but you'd be hard-pressed to find much reporting on cable TV or other current news sources about what may be a disaster for the whole of human kind. Occasional dribbles and dabs, perhaps, but certainly no front-page headline grabbing or sustained news reporting. It's a story that seems to have gone away, news-wise, even though the population clock is indeed still ticking.

How much human life can the Earth sustain . . . in terms of the ratio of population to available sustainable resources? Experts all over the world are grappling with this question. More important to you: how will this affect *your* business? In short, you will have to find creative ways to accomplish more with less. For instance, CEOs of automobile manufacturing companies would be wise to be standing by with smaller, more fuel-efficient car designs.

Diminishing Resources

A growing population will inevitably require more food, space, water, energy—and virtually every other natural resource. Yet when we look at the data, it becomes alarmingly apparent that our natural resources have already begun a downward spiral.

We must consider what will happen when less-developed countries begin to experience dwindling resources past a tolerable threshold, or when countries that have managed to develop *nuclear weapons* can't feed their populations or keep the lights on. Resource wars *will* break out when things get bad enough.

In order to thrive in coming years, we all have to educate ourselves on how diminishing resources will impact business—and then create a strategy to deal with that fact. The more aware you are of the global changes taking place, the better your chances of continued success.

An enterprising person is one who comes across a pile of scrap metal and sees the making of a wonderful sculpture. An enterprising person is one who drives through an old, decrepit part of town and sees a new housing development. An enterprising person is one who sees opportunity in all areas of life.

—Jim Rohn

Global Need for More Energy

Global energy demand is estimated to increase 58 percent over the next 25 years; and that power has to come from *somewhere* in order for civilization as we know it to thrive. Renewable energy is still in its infancy, and although the use of solar, wind, and other renewable resources is growing, we still use mostly fossil fuels—oil, coal, and natural gas—which are beginning to diminish (See Figures 1.2, 1.3 and 1.4.) There is no magic bullet that will solve our energy dilemma, and we'll likely consume anything we can get our hands on for the next two or three decades. But then what?

The more your business depends on energy, the more vulnerable you will be as energy prices continue to rise. My local electric company has raised the rates for my company's recording studio complex 14 percent in the last year—which has given us an incentive to find ways to be more efficient. We've taken some drastic measures to use less electricity, thereby lowering our bills and our carbon footprint at the same time. One of the biggest kilowatt users is our million-dollar collection of mixing consoles, recording gear, and power amps, all of which generate a lot of heat. Conventional wisdom says they must be left on 24 hours a day, and kept cool with air-conditioning whether the studios are in use or not. Going against what all the "experts" advise, I decided to turn off all equipment that wasn't being used and shut off the air-conditioning in those rooms. I've been around this type of equipment my entire life, and concluded that this was a risk worth taking. I'm happy to say not one piece of equipment—or client—has suffered. We've also gone to great

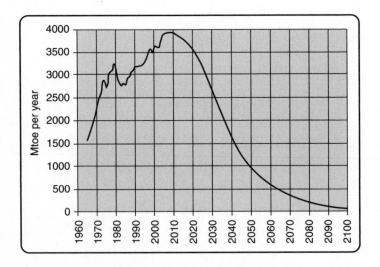

Figure 1.2   **OIL BECOMING SCARCER.**
These next three graphs show that energy is the key *limiting* natural resource that threatens economic growth. We have probably already passed the "peaks" in extracting oil, gas, and even coal, which is impacting your business right now.
Source: **http://canada.theoildrum.com/node/3091.**

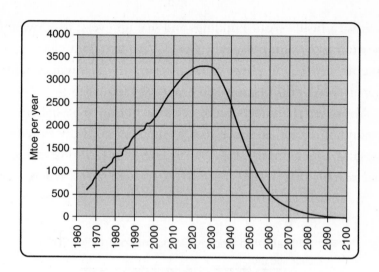

Figure 1.3 **GAS BECOMING SCARCER.**
Source: **http://canada.theoildrum.com/node/3091.**

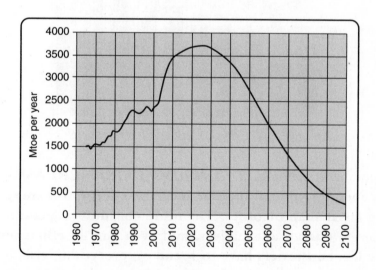

Figure 1.4 **COAL BECOMING SCARCER.**
Source: **http://canada.theoildrum.com/node/3091.**

lengths to insulate our buildings and seal up every window and door to make them practically airtight. And yes, our electric bill has gone down, and future price increases—which will certainly happen—will affect us less and less. (See Figure 1.5.)

Your electric bill has no place to go but up as global energy demand continues to grow, so start figuring out how to reduce that and other energy bills. Are there things you've deemed "necessary" that really are not? Are there areas where you

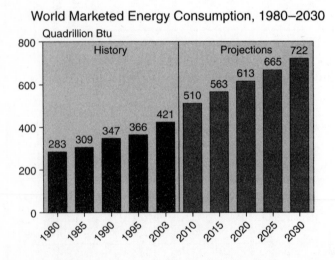

Figure 1.5 **ENERGY CONSUMPTION INCREASES. As energy *usage* continues to increase, energy *costs* are rising faster than incomes. The more consumers spend for energy, energy alternatives, and even energy efficiency, the less consumers have to spend on everything else.**
Sources: **History—Energy Information Administration (EIA), International Energy Annual 2003 (May–July 2005), www.eia.doe.gov/ iea. Projections—EIA, System for the Analysis of Global Energy Markets (2006). From http://timeforchange.org/prediction-of-energy-consumption.**

can save energy and money, or somehow combine resources? Whether you're a mammoth company like Walmart or a small start-up, there are countless actions you can take to heighten your efficiency.

Your business doesn't use much energy, you say? There are hidden energy costs about which most businesses aren't fully aware. For example, Amazon.com sells books that are delivered to customers via UPS or FedEx, whose planes and trucks need jet fuel and diesel—and lots of it. At some point, the cost of shipping those books may be too high a price to pay; only the market can decide that. But the recent introduction of the electronic book reader "Kindle" and the "Tablet" allows Amazon to ship you the content electronically for one-ten-thousandth of the energy cost of mailing the paper version (not to mention the savings in trees). Amazon is looking toward the future and adjusting its business model to be less sensitive to UPS and FedEx shipping costs. What can *your* business do?

Fragile Environment

You can't operate a profitable fishing business if there are no longer fish in the ocean, and you can't be a successful farmer if your soil can no longer supply the nutrients needed to produce a bountiful crop. You can't run a successful printing business if paper costs keep skyrocketing because trees for producing pulp are in short supply. Be it oil, silicon chips, or copy paper—just about every material your business uses comes from nature and is in limited supply. (Silicon chips are made from sand, which admittedly is plentiful, but it requires a huge amount of energy to turn plain sand into pure silicon.) It therefore makes good business sense to incorporate protecting our fragile environment into your business model so that your company can grow and prosper.

Our impact on the planet has grown by exponential proportions, and our collective technologies have made us a force of—and too often *against*—nature. You don't have to be a rocket scientist to realize that there will be a price to pay if we continue wasting limited natural resources. And with your customers paying higher prices for scarce commodities, they'll have less to spend at your business. (See Figure 1.6.)

Every company has a responsibility to come up with potential solutions. Individual people can make a difference, but *business* has the real power to start reversing many of these environmental issues. Millions of people vote with their pocketbooks every day in an effort to encourage businesses to provide environmentally friendly products. Each time people vote, they create another opportunity for some person or company to serve that customer and follow their lead.

Though these problems can seem daunting, creating successful sustainable business models goes hand in hand with resolving many of these global issues. However, before we can start making educated decisions on how to change the way we approach business, we must identify the specific challenges that we're now facing. And in the following chapters, we do just that.

Once you commit your business to becoming more efficient, leaner, meaner, more creative, and more passionate in your mission, your company will flourish. In the process, your bottom line—and the planet's—will become *significantly* healthier—and your company's bottom line will be healthier, too.

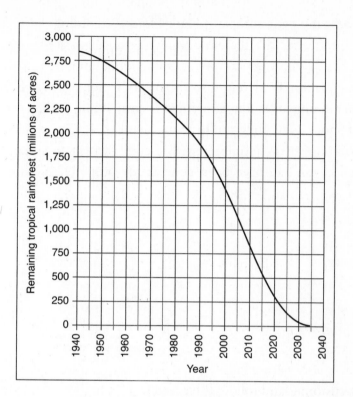

Figure 1.6 **REMAINING TROPICAL RAINFOREST.**
Rainforest destruction is symbolic of how we humans
treat our environment. Those consequences will not only
impact the earth's climate, but the business climate as well.
Source: **http://tropicalhardwoods.com/htm/tree_owners_news/**
charts/rainforest_remaining_small.gif.

Sustainable Practices = Sustainable Companies

In the following chapters we'll take a look at what some
forward-thinking companies are doing to achieve sustainability and higher profitability. I'll share stories about how I

brought my own company, Dark Horse Recording, back from the brink after the technology revolution devastated many of the best recording studios in the world, and how part of that equation is in response to the four global issues I listed earlier. Companies like Stonyfield Farms, Trader Joe's, Timberland Shoes, New Belgium Brewing, and FLOR Carpet Tiles are all running their businesses with a commitment to sustainable practices, and all have been consistently profitable, as you can be, too.

2 | Change Is a Choice

You better start swimming
Or you'll sink like a stone
For the times they are a-changin'

— Bob Dylan

Bob Dylan hit the nail on the head with those lyrics. Forty years ago—while Dylan was recording albums like *Highway 61 Revisited* and *Blonde on Blonde*—the United States was experiencing an explosion of creativity and change with the emergence of drugs, sex, rock and roll, and the raging war in Vietnam. Yet looking back, the changes and transformations of the 1960s, 1970s, 1980s, and even the 1990s seem mild in comparison to what we're contending with now.

Today, those changes are accelerating exponentially, often with dark and ominous repercussions. However, along with change comes opportunity. Navigating these times of constant transformations can bring out our very best—as long as we nurture a positive mindset and attitude.

Better the Devil You Know Than
the Devil You Don't

Remember the phrase, "Change we can believe in"? That was
the platform on which Barack Obama ran for President. In
every speech he gave, he consistently outlined his vision for
change,.. and health care reform was near the top of his list.
Although it's clear that our current health care system isn't really
working and despite the fact that the United States is the world's
leading economic superpower, we rank only 37 in the world
in terms of health care. Nonetheless, U.S. citizens seem to be
terrified with the uncertainty that accompanies trying it any other
way—even though our health care system is bloated and broken.
The prevailing mindset seems to be, "better the devil you know
than the devil you don't." But I think we all know on some level
that the devil you *don't* know is the real danger.

> *There can only be one solution to any problem: a change in attitude*
> *and in consciousness.*
>
> —Gregg Braden

"I Hate Change"

One of the greatest pleasures in my life is the long horse rides
I share with my daughter Savannah. Often, we get started at
sunrise before the day gets under way. Fortunately, we have several generous neighbors who allow us to ride on their adjoining
farms. Just imagine rolling picturesque grassy fields outlined by
dense forest providing seemingly endless riding paths. It's some
of the most beautiful countryside in all of Tennessee.

Over time, we've locked onto a route that is so comfortable and familiar that the horses can practically navigate it with their eyes closed. Recently, as we were preparing for one of our early morning rides, I proposed that we try the route backward. Savannah's reply . . . "Dad, no way. You know *I hate change!*" Out of the mouths of babes . . . I was reminded that even teenagers fundamentally resist anything that's different. Apparently it's just human nature to hate change!

The truth is that we are afraid of uncertainty, of stepping into unknown territory, because it requires that we view things differently. And what if these new things don't work out? What if our ideas are rejected, or if we don't fit in? I recently acquired a book titled *Change is Good . . . You Go First*. What a great title! It sums up the way so many of us feel about change; it's perfectly fine, as long as someone else does the changing first.

> *The public have insatiable curiosity to know everything—except what's worth knowing.*
>
> —Oscar Wilde

Change, Change, and More Change

For the first 20 years of my adult life, I was a touring musician and recording artist. After releasing six albums on smaller labels, I eventually signed with RCA records.

Standing in the RCA building in New York and signing my contract I thought my days of financially treading water were almost over. At one point I was informed that RCA spent $700,000 for the recording and promoting of my album, *Electric Cinema*, with the idea that we were swinging for the bleachers. In other words: the company strategy was to promote the record like crazy, and we would either hit a home run or strike out. But, if an album isn't soon flying off the shelves, they won't even keep it on life support. There is no middle ground.

That was the case with *Electric Cinema*. We had one minor radio hit, but it wasn't enough to kick sales into high gear. Two years later, I was dropped from the label. I was turning forty and was broke; I had no choice but to evolve or die. For the first time in 20 years, I had to consider new career options. I was forced into changing and that's a tough position to be in.

That experience caused me to have a lot of compassion for anyone who's hit a similar wall with their current career path, but fears leaping into unknown waters. However, sometimes life simply *happens*, and something—or someone—pushes us off that diving board. It's uncomfortable, humbling, and scary, but at the same time, it can be exhilarating and liberating.

That's exactly how I felt when I decided to start my own business. Although I kept telling myself that I wanted something different, my identity was completely wrapped up in being a recording artist. Of course, it was frightening to think of creating a business that depended on technical excellence *well* beyond my understanding. I wondered—even if I *could* find the resources to create the studio and make it work—how would I find customers who would pay to use it? At the time, it all seemed completely overwhelming.

During these tumultuous times, you will be bombarded with unexpected changes in the form of setbacks and adversities that arise with greater frequency. How you respond to those changes will determine your level of success.

Opening Our Doors for Business

When I started Dark Horse Recording, I felt more pressure, anxiety, and fear than at any other point that I can remember in my life. Change rarely comes in the shape that we would prefer, but we usually become stronger and wiser from the experience once we get through it. When we're faced with a tremendous challenge, we often find strengths we didn't even know we had.

Truth be told, I was only willing to accept a career change because my back was up against the wall. I had bills due, kids to feed, and a mortgage to pay; I really didn't have much choice. When I first opened my doors for business, Dark Horse was nothing more than a small no-nonsense studio attached to a run-down, "green acres"–type house I had just managed to buy before getting dropped from RCA. I had used up every resource I could get my hands on to get this far.

It took every ounce of courage and creativity I had to scrape together the resources to bring Dark Horse into existence. For three and a half years, I worked every day as a carpenter, bartering for labor, and selling everything that wasn't nailed down. I took out lines of credit at hardware stores and lumberyards, and I managed to run up $134,000 on my credit cards before finally getting a bank loan. The pressure was intense, and there was no turning back. I was only going to achieve success by finding a way to move forward, each and every day. During those tough times, dealing with constant change became business as usual.

Adapting to change is more important than any other factor in achieving success.

Make Money Now, Organize Later

Many years ago, author Mark H. McCormack wrote a book entitled *What They Don't Teach You at Harvard Business School*. One
bit of advice he gave in reference to starting a business was "make
money now, organize later." As many small business owners can
attest, sometimes the only way to get a fledgling business off the
ground is to just *get started,* to take action immediately. In other
words, just do it.

McCormack's advice stayed with me over the years. Dark
Horse opened as merely a shell of what is expected from a truly
world-class recording facility. I had a single studio attached to
my log home with only the bare minimum of equipment to
get by. It was a far cry from the four well-equipped studios in
a complex that now operates seven days a week with staff and
interns to keep things together. I discovered, however, that most
of the A-list producers and engineers already had so much gear
they brought with them that they were willing to overlook my
lack of auxiliary equipment.

What made Dark Horse different from other studios was
not the high-tech equipment (or lack thereof) but the *ambi-
ence*. Every room was rustic, with skylights and oversize plate-
glass windows overlooking the countryside. I advertised it as
"secluded and private"; code words for "off the beaten path
and hard to find." But to recording artists it meant a peaceful
place they could work without annoyances and interruptions.
Seclusion and privacy won out over the high-tech equipment I
couldn't afford and didn't have. Over the next five years, I built
up Dark Horse in quality and scope. In the process, I erected
an almost 10,000-square-foot building from scratch that would
house an additional three studios. The challenge was finding the

resources to keep the project moving forward. It seemed as if change was the only constant. A decade later Dark Horse has become quite the success story, but each small accomplishment required that our team be able to manage *change*. Although we became more technically savvy over the years (and today operate some of the most advanced recording equipment available anywhere in the world), our team focused more on the artist's comfort than on the gear in the racks. The artists control where they want to record, and they want to be comfortable when they create.

After our first five years in business the recording industry began to change, and forced me to do the same. I couldn't postpone it, ignore it, or hide from it. Forced change is the hardest. Change is easier if it's gradual and you control the schedule. It is cheaper, safer, and far easier on the soul to look ahead and anticipate where markets will be in three to five years and adjust to them in your own time frame than to wait for change to be forced on you.

Staying Focused on What Matters

In December 1972 an Eastern Airlines L1011 was at 2,000 feet on final approach into Miami. One of the next-to-last steps prior to landing was lowering the landing gear. When the nose gear light failed to illuminate, confirming that the landing gear was "down and locked," the flight engineer left the cockpit and headed into the avionics bay beneath to check on the mechanism. In the meantime, both the pilot and copilot began fiddling with the landing gear light, trying to see if the bulb was fully plugged in or if they could somehow fix it. Because they were focused on the "quick fix" of a *light bulb*, no one was actually flying the plane as it slowly, but gradually, descended. An altitude-warning chime sounded in the cockpit, but both the pilot and copilot ignored it, apparently frustrated that they couldn't get the indicator light to work. Finally, the copilot noticed that something was wrong:

Copilot: "We did something to the altitude."
Pilot: "What?"
Copilot: "We're still at 2,000 feet, right?"

The pilot's response (and last words) were "Hey, what's happening here?" Seconds later, the plane crashed into the Everglades, killing 101 people.

The National Transportation Safety Board investigation noted that the cause of the crash was due to "the failure of the flight crew to monitor the flight instruments during the final four minutes of flight, and to detect an unexpected descent soon enough to prevent impact with the ground. Preoccupation with a malfunction of the nose landing gear position indicating system distracted the crew's attention from the instruments and allowed the descent to go unnoticed."

In the U.S. mainstream media, we focus far too much on the famous and the trivial and not enough on the critical and the important. This is a reflection of our fascination with pop culture and spills over into our politics, government, and even carries over into business. You'd think serious-minded businesspeople would know better. But remember: they were "people" before they ever became "businesspeople," and most are products of their cultural surroundings. Too often, too many business leaders allow themselves to get sidetracked from mission critical issues and end up focusing instead on trivial problems. In some businesses today, nobody's "flying the plane." Don't be one of them. Figure out what your business's mission critical functions are and stay focused on them. Don't let your business's "descent go unnoticed." Don't wait until someone has to ask you: "Hey, what's happening here?"

3 | Rearranging the Chairs on the Titanic

We're bombarded with sensationalized news stories on a daily basis. It doesn't matter if we're in an airport, in our car, or in the comfort of our own homes, we're hit from every direction. We receive vivid details about the latest disaster in Iraq at the breakfast table, or hear about a tragedy on the freeway while sitting at our desks. Of course, it's important that we know about these stories. But we're so used to hearing about the unbelievable and the unthinkable that we barely have time to react. We've become so desensitized to it all, and have our own, more pressing personal issues staring us right in the face. We have families to support and businesses to run. It's easy to push these overwhelming national and global issues down to the bottom of our endless list of concerns.

A pessimist sees the difficulty in every opportunity; an optimist sees the opportunity in every difficulty.

—Winston Churchill

Change Can Occur Overnight

Despite our tendency to expect warnings for life-altering events, dramatic changes in our world and personal lives can occur overnight. Consider the fall of Communism in Russia and the collapse of the Berlin wall in the late 1980s. No one—not even the CIA—suspected a monolithic government like the Soviet Union could crumble so swiftly. Consider, however, a small crack in a dam that at first appears harmless. That tiny crack is under so much pressure that it soon propagates across the entire width of the dam until it disintegrates. It's incredibly arrogant for us to think that our American way of life is exempt from the possibility of a similar fate. Throughout recorded human history, some 3,825 societies (that we know of) have collapsed. In many cases, those societies had found ways to exploit every conceivable natural resource and then feed off the local ecology, thriving only while they *grew*. Once they were no longer able to *expand*, they became the victims of their own success. The Roman Empire, for example, continued expanding until the very breadth of its borders proved impossible to defend. For business people to not consider the bigger picture would be remiss—to say the least.

The leaders of tomorrow are the ones who recognize the gravity of each issue we face today, and who will incorporate that knowing into action to make their businesses more sustainable.

We're All on the Same (Sinking) Ship

The facts are clear: we are on a ship, and it's taking on more water every second. The convergence of the aforementioned issues leave little doubt that, if left unchecked, our ship *will sink*. The difference between our ship's predicament and the *Titanic's* is that we aren't quite sure how long we have. Although the *Titanic's* disaster was immediate and irreversible, our situation provides us some time to correct the ship's direction and avoid the iceberg if we recognize the warning signs and act quickly enough.

Globally, we bicker endlessly and fight wars over ideology and oil. In the United States, we focus on trivia and drama. If we can't find a way to focus on the real "big picture," we aren't going to have anything to fight over anymore. It's as if we're rearranging the chairs on the deck of the *Titanic*, even though the ship is clearly sinking.

Can one person really make a difference? In the late 1950s a popular tranquilizer and painkiller was being used in Europe to treat everything from insomnia to morning sickness. By the early 1960s a U.S. drug company, Richardson Merrell, wanted to market the drug in the United States and applied to the FDA for permission. Typically, drugs in widespread use in Europe were easily and routinely approved for use in the United States. During the approval process, a single FDA inspector, Dr. Frances Kelsey—acting alone—on her own hunch, blocked the approval of the popular drug. It wasn't a team, a group, or a committee; it was one determined woman.

Undoubtedly, Dr. Kelsey was under pressure to grant approval. After all, the drug was highly successful and highly profitable in Europe and the United States was a big market for new drugs (still is). In the meantime, the drug company gave away a few samples to doctors with the understanding the drug was "still under investigation." Nonetheless, Dr. Kelsey refused to budge. The drug Dr. Kelsey single-handedly turned down was called *Thalidomide*.

Never heard of Thalidomide? It turns out that the drug that was given to pregnant women for morning sickness caused severe birth defects. During the period Dr. Kelsey stood her ground, more than 2,500 Thalidomide babies were born in Germany alone, and thousands more across Europe but only 17 in the United States (from the physician's samples the company handed out). In 1962, President Kennedy gave Dr. Kelsey an award for blocking the sale in the United States of Thalidomide. That same year Congress passed laws requiring more stringent safety tests before a drug can be approved for sale in the United States. Because of Dr. Kelsey, thousands of American children were spared the horrors of Thalidomide (and European regulators took note and eventually banned it there, too). So, can one person really make a difference? Do I really have to answer that?

The American Dream

Don't get me wrong; I am proud to be an American. But I believe we've lost our way in recent years. Our country cannot continue to simply rearrange the chairs on deck; that is, make small, incremental changes that really don't have much collective effect. We're never going to turn our economy around by continuing to repeat the same things we've always done; we have to focus on the bigger picture. Remember, our country's dream didn't just *happen*; we the people *made* it happen. Countless U.S. citizens have made the ultimate sacrifice over the last two centuries to help create and preserve an ideal that's often taken for granted.

The United States was founded on the principle that any person can achieve success through thrift and hard work.

People could rise up from harsh and impoverished circumstances, create an extraordinary life for themselves, and prosper.
That notion inspired us to become one of the most envied—and
certainly most powerful—nations in the world. We're privi-
leged to be able to speak and worship without restriction, and
choose our friends no matter what race, creed, or color they
might be. Living in the United States offers us the opportunity to educate our children in public or private schools,
or even at home. As adults, we are encouraged to continue
learning; we can travel freely and visit whomever and wherever
we choose.

Though I'll always be grateful to live in a land where individual expression is every person's right, I believe that the promise
that shaped our nation has now come to symbolize prosperity
in the form of materialism and greed. In our pursuit of bigger
cars, fancier homes, and designer clothes, we've gotten caught
up in conspicuous consumption. The American dream has begun to gradually erode; and it's been replaced with a "get rich
quick" philosophy. Perhaps unconsciously, we've developed a
short-term focused, "having it all" mentality. And the fact that
these philosophies have become so pervasive and "normal" to
us, the idea of shifting our views and doing business a different
way is difficult for us to grasp.

We cannot continue to extract these finite resources to sat-
isfy our global need for more with little or no consideration
for the future. We live at a time when we humans will finally have to confront the fact we are about to encounter
some hard physical limits.

Turning a Blind Eye (Why No One Cares)

It's no secret that health care, the energy crunch, the economy, terrorism, and the environment are *such* monumental issues; so why aren't more people eager to become part of the solution? I get the impression that many people don't believe their actions would make a difference, either because they have limited resources, or because they see their efforts as futile. Or maybe they don't get involved because no one has ever challenged them to do so. Either way, it's easier to turn a blind eye to these issues and continue to focus on our personal pursuits.

The Most Adaptable Species on the Planet

It's simple: we accept the lifestyle to which we've become accustomed. It's been said that humans are the most adaptable species on the planet. That's a good thing, because we may well have no choice but to "adapt" by downsizing our lifestyles in the near future. We must use our unique ability to quickly evolve to embrace the changes taking place around us.

Think about the millions of people who call Manhattan home and accept the fact that they live in extremely small quarters. Many of those city dwellers have not only adapted to these circumstances; they wouldn't have it any other way. Given the choice to live in a sprawling suburb or in the country, they would likely choose to stay right where they are. On the other hand, my four children grew up on a 10-acre farm with plenty of room to stretch out and explore. My home and business is on the same property, so my children are accustomed to the sound of drums and electric guitars coming from the adjacent studios.

Seven days a week, there are both musicians and horses on the property, and this has been a daily part of my kids' lives, and the only reality they've ever known. Therefore, it's hard to imagine how they might react if our family was suddenly transplanted to Tokyo and forced to live in a 400-square-foot apartment. But the truth is that we would soon adjust to living in ultra-tight quarters, and after a while we wouldn't give it another thought.

One thing is for certain: we cannot continue to work and play with that same wasteful mentality as we have in the past. Most of our environmental problems exist because we have not made solving them a high enough priority. Moving forward, we must give these challenges our utmost attention, as we create ways to adapt to the threats that are presenting themselves. Only then will our commerce thrive.

On a Scale of 1 to 10

We know that although we're *capable* of change, we usually need a good reason to accept and go forth with it. Do most people consider resources and the environment a good enough reason to change their actions, their business plans, even their careers? Unfortunately, not in most cases.

I remember back a couple of years ago when I called my sisters Laura and Beth and asked each of them this question: "On a scale of 1 to 10, how much does global warming concern you?" One of them said "one"; and the other, "zero." Now, both of my sisters graduated with BAs in journalism from Baylor University and are sharp as tacks, so I can only surmise that America's indifference to such staggering issues comes from a collective herd mentality in which all of us are caught. If the herd is grazing peacefully in the field then everything must be okay—no need to worry. If no one else is concerned, then why should I be? Intelligence and education don't necessarily translate into concern about issues that will ultimately and forcefully shape our lives and those of every generation to come.

The Last Thing We Need

Most of us feel immense pressure from the obligations and stresses that it takes just to keep our homes, hold on to our jobs and businesses, and raise our families. And even though the *last* thing many of us need is another challenge, we unfortunately don't have a choice on this one. We are living in the "information age," a time of instant access to an almost infinite amount of information. We know how our minds work; we know about human behavior, nutrition, and depression, and that there's no such thing as a winnable war anymore—certainly not a winnable *nuclear* war. Technological advances have allowed us to accomplish amazing feats that have made our lives incredibly easy. You would think that humans would be totally committed to doing whatever it takes to live long and peacefully prosper. While the *Titanic* was sinking, the orchestra continued to play waltzes. Are we being lulled when we should be avoiding the icebergs ahead or patching the holes in the ship?

We must evolve whether we like it or not; the longer we delay, the more difficult it will be to keep the ship afloat. We can no longer continue to reshuffle the same "we've always done it this way" policies and expect to profit. Regurgitating the same tired ideas won't keep your customers coming back in the door. If your ship has a breach in the hull, that's where your focus needs to be; not on rearranging the deck chairs.

> What are some fundamental changes you can make to strengthen and secure the longevity of your company? If you are in the retail business, stop simply reorganizing the way the shelves are stocked, and start finding creative, low-cost ways to add value to your customers' shopping experience. How can you secure their loyalty to your establishment? Most importantly, begin rethinking how you can implement those ideas more efficiently. This will offer your business a tremendous opportunity to move beyond rearranging the same old chairs so you can start fixing the ruptured hull that's causing the ship to sink in the first place.

4 | Reinvention

Many of life's failures are people who did not realize how close they were to success when they gave up.

—Thomas Edison

Your company's success in this century depends on you and your colleagues' abilities to rethink, restructure, reinspire, and reinvent your brand. There have been countless companies throughout history—Sony, Xerox, Kodak, and AT&T, to name a few—who have risked reinventing themselves and thus revitalized their business model.

However, there's no one I can think of in recent history who has mastered the art of reinvention like Madonna. Legendary for her relentless work ethic, marketing genius, and a talent for consistently re-creating her pop star persona, she even dubbed one of her tours the "reinvention" tour. Whether you're in the music business or own a widget factory, Madonna can actually teach you some valuable lessons. She's experienced unquestionable success in the entertainment industry, but she is all business, and a force to be reckoned with. I would go so far as to compare her work ethic to that of the best corporate CEOs, because she clearly understands you absolutely *must* evolve—or your business (or career) will die—when it comes to professional

37

longevity. She's always fresh, and even after 25 years her audience has continued to expand as she delivers the goods year after year.

You might still be wondering—what *exactly* does Madonna's success have to with *my* business? Everything. She has adapted to her surroundings for a quarter of a century, single-mindedly overcame some fairly daunting obstacles, and has chosen time and again to change. She has kept her business relevant and profitable through a relentless pursuit of reinvention and adaptation.

> Whether you're a small business owner, entrepreneur, or CEO of a major corporation, the challenges remain the same. You must relentlessly search for ways to differentiate and reinvent yourself.

Detergent

Reinvention is essentially about adapting to change, and another excellent example of this is detergent—yes, detergent. Analyzing the evolution of this product makes a clear point about how to modify your product—and company—with changing market demands. Most detergent comes in large boxes or bucket-size plastic containers, leading many to wonder why it's packaged with so much unnecessary filler. The reason is that a customer's potential perception of "more" makes the detergent more sellable. Consumers are suckers for "bigger is better," so even though companies like Tide or Dash could easily produce condensed detergent in packages a fraction of the size, that would hurt potential sales two ways. First, purchasers would likely feel that they are getting less of a product. Even if a smaller concentrated box at the same price advertised that it would wash 60 loads compared to the larger box advertising 50, many consumers would still choose the larger box. Second, with out the bigger boxes they would add space on the shelf. Although condensing their product would reduce the cost of packaging and shipping, the big box on the shelf serves as a great point-of-purchase billboard. Have you ever noticed how detergent takes up nearly an aisle's worth of space in the grocery store?

Tide and Dash know all too well that bigger packaging is more expensive to produce, store, and ship. Only once those detergent-producing companies think the buying public will purchase the condensed soap just as readily as condensed soup, will they shift their focus to only offer the smaller version. Other companies must solve similar conundrums in order to remain viable, and be forced to evolve or die. So here's the question: would you rather be on the offensive or defensive side of this equation? It's only a matter of time until there will be a tipping point, and big boxes of detergent will become as passé as the transistor radio.

Vinyl Records to CDs

Several decades ago, record stores were stocked wall to wall with 12-by-12 inch cardboard sleeves. That large size was the perfect way to showcase the album artwork, a major factor in highlighting the product and luring the customer to pick it up and buy it. When CDs first arrived on the scene, they were packaged in large—and wasteful—6-inch-wide by 12-inch-tall parcels to offer that bigger display experience. Two CDs exhibited side by side took the same space as an album did, which allowed stores to maintain the same racks and shelves. However, once someone bought a CD, they then had to tear the box open to get at the item inside, which was enclosed in a much smaller plastic jewel case. It didn't take long for that concept to give way to a smaller, more efficient, cheaper, and less wasteful form of packaging. Now you're likely to see a large point-of-purchase display with large posters of the CD cover along with stacks of small CDs.

The aforementioned detergent companies are working on similar marketing ideas. In a few years, you're likely to see brightly lit animated display screens in the aisles of grocery stores (which will ironically be about the size of today's giant-size detergent boxes). But the new display will entice you to buy the more petite, concentrated detergent package. Detergent sales will not suffer, but the marketing and packaging formula will make more sense than today's version.

Companies must continue to consider how to sell their products with a "smaller-size box" approach, just as record companies developed ways to sell music without a foot-square, trendily decorated album sleeve.

> Reinventing yourself is a balancing act between maintaining brand consistency and keeping things fresh. People have always been attracted to a combination of certainty and uncertainty.

Apple Computer

Reinvention is critical to increasing the value of your business. It's a paradoxical balance between etching your brand into your customers' minds while simultaneously coming up with fresh, creative products. No company has done a better job of this than Apple Computer. Apple has continually adapted to global and cultural trends by creating cutting-edge products and staying well ahead of the curve.

I'll never forget the first time I saw U2 advertising the iPod on TV; I just didn't get it. Although I own several recording studios and therefore (at least, should) have a better-than-average understanding of how music is recorded, I couldn't comprehend the idea of putting hundreds of songs on a device smaller than a billfold—and with no knobs, too. But Steve Jobs was thinking light years ahead; and as we've all come to realize, the iPod has become a category of one—and has literally revolutionized the music industry.

It almost seems as though Jobs observes the current trends of the world around him and asks questions like, "What if a cell phone could also be a digital audio player, a camera phone with text messaging and visual voicemail, an Internet client with e-mail and web browsing functions, and video capability—and fit in your pocket, too? Wouldn't that be nice?" So he built the iPhone, which has thus far sold 22 million units. Even though the model I own is 18 months old and works perfectly, it has already been replaced several times over, as Apple continues to release more powerful versions with updated features. The iPhone continues to *evolve*.

Apple has done an amazing job of continually reinventing themselves since they were first established in 1976. Year after year, the company has introduced new ways to advance computer technology. They have not only adapted to the transformations of the world around them, they've brilliantly managed to *forecast* these changes and develop products accordingly. Apple is now taking this adaptation one step further by becoming more environmentally friendly with the MacBook Air—their greenest product to date. This computer consumes the least amount of electricity of any Mac, and has countless features—like a highly recyclable, mercury-free aluminum enclosure, a mercury-free LCD display with arsenic-free glass, and largely recyclable, low-volume packaging—designed to reduce environmental impact throughout the product's lifecycle.

In addition to presenting a fantastic product, this makes perfect business sense. As the passionate owner of a MacBook Air with which I regularly travel, I am constantly receiving comments on planes and in airports by people who are struck by how *thin* it is. They always ask me how I like it, and I enjoy telling them about how I'm able to slip my computer in the side pouch of my suitcase as if it were a magazine. My infatuation with this product becomes quite obvious when I start telling them about all the other features and how green it is, too. What goal could be more rewarding than to have millions of people passionately advertising your products for you? (And by the way, Steve Jobs is worth more than 5 billion dollars—living proof that it pays to reinvent!)

> Constantly rethink how to keep your brand relevant, consumers loyal, competitors minimized, and revenues growing.

Snuggies

If you've ever seen those infomercials for Snuggies—the "blanket with sleeves"—I'll bet it's brought a smile to your face. These ads show happy consumers wearing Snuggies at picnics, eating popcorn on the couch, reading the paper in bed, or at sporting events cheering and high-fiving each other while dressed in what appear to be oversize fleece blankets with sleeves. Some of these spots are so cheesy and entertaining that one might easily assume that they're a *Saturday Night Live* spoof with actors who look like members of a church choir who forgot to take off their robes after the service.

So when I heard Allstar Products Group of Hawthorne, New York had sold 4 million of these, well, you could have knocked me over with a feather. This product has truly transcended advertising and become part of pop culture. There's an official Snuggies fan page with more than 15,000 fans. You can watch them on YouTube with nearly 300 parody videos posted, including one titled "The Cult of the Snuggie" that's enjoyed more than 900,000 views. There are more than 250 sites dedicated to either loving or hating them—such as SnuggieSightings.com—where fans post photos, videos, and "news." There are even Snuggie drinking games on college campuses where students take a swig every time a Snuggie commercial airs, and Snuggie bar crawls in cities where people travel from one pub to another clad in their "blankets with sleeves."

And just as it seemed that things couldn't get any more surreal—now there are Snuggies for dogs! After all, "many Snuggie customers are also dog owners, and no one wants the owners feeling bad about jealous glances from their pets." Well then. I could go on, but I promise to stop and make my point: we could all learn a thing or two from Scott Boilen, Allstar's president and CEO and creator of this crazy product. Allstar is continually reinventing themselves, and although you can say what you want about their commercials, when someone comes up with something so unique that *4 million people* buy it, well, they must be doing something right. In addition to buying Snuggies from infomercial ads, consumers can now find Snuggies at Bed Bath and Beyond, Walgreens, CVS, and Walmart. Now *that's* big business.

The Beatles

Earlier in the chapter, I spotlighted Madonna's remarkable mastery at reinventing herself. The Beatles are another iconic group with an extraordinary ability to constantly change and set trends that permeated every aspect of U.S. culture. These four musicians did much more than just set musical trends; their influence crosses over into the business world as well, and if you were an entrepreneur during the mid-1960s, there was opportunity to be had.

On February 9, 1964, the Beatles made their U.S. debut on *The Ed Sullivan Show,* and from that moment on, pop culture was never the same. Imagine that you owned a barbershop at a time when every American kid suddenly wanted to look like the Beatles. You would either have to reinvent your styling techniques, or resist change and likely take a revenue hit. Some barbers saw where the trends were headed and transitioned their barbershops into men's salons—making even more money than they ever did as a barber. Additionally, guitar manufacturers like Gretch, Rickenbacker, or Hoffner—the brands the Beatles played—would have done well to grab this opportunity and run to respond to the thousands of kids knocking down their doors for these products.

Malcolm Gladwell attributes much of the Beatles' unprecedented success in his book *Outliers* to the enormous amount of time they played and rehearsed together for years before ever signing their first record deal. He calls it "the 10,000-hour rule," although I disagree with his conclusion. As the owner of a recording complex and a recording artist with 10 albums of my own out, I have seen hundreds of acts with amazing talent. But that's not the reason the Beatles were the most influential band in history. Think about it. With limited technology and no blueprint from earlier bands to follow, the Beatles quickly differentiated themselves from groups like the Dave Clark Five and Herman's Hermits by evolving . . . nearly from day one! The band was in creative overdrive 24 hours a day 7 . . . oops, 8 days a week in an effort to keep themselves and their music fresh. With each new album they would risk their popularity by pushing the envelope with their look and musical evolution. By the time they recorded their *Sgt. Pepper's Lonely Hearts Club Band* album, they had morphed into a band that looked different and sounded different. The Beatles were second to none when it came to reinventing themselves. What makes them so amazing is the extraordinary journey they embarked on in such a short period of time. And we all went along for the ride. The leap in style and content from *Please Please Me* in 1963, to *Sgt. Pepper* in 1967, to the *White Album* in 1968 was nothing short of extraordinary. Their instincts were to push the limits, step out on a limb, and evolve. In doing so they created the most enduring career of any band in history.

5

Every Innovative Business Has a Great Story

So what do we do? Anything - something. So long as we don't just sit there. If we screw it up, start over. Try something else. If we wait until we've satisfied all the uncertainties, it may be too late.

—Lee Iacocca

Blockbuster versus Netflix

In the early 1990s, leading cable company Continental Cablevision was trying to decide if, when, and how to get into video on demand. Doing so would provide their customers with the ability to watch any movie they wanted at any time. The company needed to decide whether to go ahead and invest in analog video on demand, or wait until their systems were digital, thus making it easier to host the service. They sent resident technical guru Bill Schleyer to Japan to scope out what new technologies might be available. Schleyer returned with a small CD-like disc,

47

and plopped it down on the table in front of his team. The
disc wasn't a CD, though. It was a *DVD*—one of the first any
Americans had ever seen—and it contained *an entire movie.*

Schleyer warned his colleagues to hold off with any analog
video-on-demand plans, and advised them to wait until their
systems were digital. Why the decision? "These things," he
simply said, "You can mail out." VHS cassettes were too bulky
and fragile to mail, but DVDs could easily and cheaply be sent
in a plain envelope for about 30 cents. Schleyer saved his company from an expensive technological mistake by realizing that
DVDs would likely be delivered by mail someday; and "someday" turned out to be roughly the year 1995. The Harvard Business School grad quickly grasped that a whole movie packaged
that compactly and lightly would be simple to send via the plain
old post office for the price of a postage stamp. Therefore, any
competing technology—like digital video on demand—would
have to work at a similar delivery cost.

Video stores were cutting-edge venues when the first Blockbuster opened in Dallas in 1985, and quickly become the biggest
purveyor of movies at the time. I remember making several trips
a week to the one in my neighborhood with my children to
rent movies for family night in the days when movies were on
bulky VHS tapes. To rent one, you had to drive to a Blockbuster
store to select your movie, and you had to bring it back *on time.*
The system worked well, and Blockbuster was, for a time, highly
profitable.

However, the inconveniences with renting from Blockbuster
were making sure the tapes were rewound and turned back in
on time. If you slipped up, they would sock you with a fine.
So when Silicon Valley programmer Reed Hastings was forced
to pay one too many late fees for failing to return movies on

time, his irritation became the impetus that prompted him to create a better system. Hastings partnered with Marc Randolph in 1997 to found Netflix—a company based on the idea that consumers could pick out their movies online and receive them via mail on a DVD. Netflix amassed 1 million subscribers in less than four years, and had shipped 1 billion movies within eight years. Through Netflix, Hastings had developed an innovative approach to movie rentals whose time had come. And today, Netflix delivers movies not only by mail, but also over the digital broadband networks Bill Schleyer helped to create.

> *In times of change, learners inherit the earth; while the learned find themselves beautifully equipped to deal with a world that no longer exists.*
>
> —Eric Hoffer

Twelve years since its inception, Netflix has crossed the milestone of shipping their 2-billionth movie. Blockbuster has some billions to talk about, too, those are unfortunately in operating losses, as the movie rental giant recently announced it was closing 960 stores.

Blockbuster was making money hand over fist renting VHS tapes from brick-and-mortar retail locations in the 1990s, so it had little reason to change its successful business model. The company eventually woke up and attempted to copy Netflix's business model, but most observers now think it is too late. A spokesperson for Blockbuster admitted that the company is now asking questions like, "Can we work with landlords? Can we remodel or refresh? What are things we can do to help stores that are on the brink of closing?" In reality, Blockbuster should have been asking those questions 10 years ago. If Blockbuster doesn't come up with something more innovative soon, they may well become a part of video history like the VHS tape itself.

However, the lesson here isn't a case of Blockbuster's management being asleep at the wheel, as many company insiders did attempt to shift the organization's business model. Successful companies are notoriously hard to change. After all, why should they, when they are making lots of cash doing what they are doing? They know it's working now, and the environmental changes that some predict in some distant future might never happen anyway. But the problem with this mentality is that corporations that don't vigilantly watch for signs of change will be replaced by other corporations who *do*—and someone else will and become the next Netflix.

> To be innovative, you will have to navigate through some business paradoxes, as you create ways to conserve and become more efficient, while at the same time accelerating growth.

"I'm Going into Business for Myself"

Once upon a time there was a quaint little town nestled in a beautiful valley. The streets were lined with picturesque storybook houses shaded by towering oak and maple trees. In the afternoons you could see children playing in the streets and couples walking, much like a scene from a Norman Rockwell painting. Then one day, a crusty, free-spirited, unemployed old-timer named Fred wandered into town and made himself at home. Once news of his arrival spread, an emergency town hall meeting was called to discuss just what the town was to do about their new and unwelcome resident. They concluded after about an hour of deliberation that it was unacceptable to have an un-employed vagrant around town. So they decided to give Fred a job polishing the old cannon in the town square so that he could be considered a respectable citizen.

Everything seemed to be going along fine for the next six months—until the day that Fred showed up at one of the monthly town meetings to announce that he was quitting. "Why would you want to quit?" they asked. He replied with great satis-faction, "I've been saving my money, I bought my own cannon, and I'm going into business for myself!"

That's the definition of a true entrepreneur: someone who must work for him or herself at all costs.

Excuses are the nails used to build a house of failure.
—Don Wilder

Born to Be an Entrepreneur

My career as an entrepreneur started out a bit like Fred's. When I was 12 years old I went out and bought my own cannon and went into business for myself, except my cannon came in the form of a lawn mower. I began mowing a half-dozen lawns within a two-block radius of my home in a middle-class neighborhood in Fort Worth, Texas. The following summer that number doubled, and my typical fee was $5 per lawn. I began plowing my earnings into a garage full of power tools for woodwork, and used my newfound wealth to begin a second career building bookshelves and coffee tables for friends and neighbors. By the time I was 15, I had learned to build speaker cabinets and rock-and-roll sound systems. I ran ads in the local paper publicizing my services, and orders for speaker systems came pouring in. Almost every garage band in town was using speakers that were built in *my* garage.

Being a young entrepreneur is an education in and of itself. You grow up fast and develop a healthy dose of self-reliance along with a tremendous work ethic. When adversities arise and you experience setbacks, you quickly learn to adapt and to think on your feet.

Whether you are a young entrepreneur or the CEO of a large organization, one thing is for certain . . . your business's success will depend on your ability to adapt to change. The recent sour economy has derailed millions of careers. Most people who run small businesses are struggling just to stay ahead, and many are rightly focused on the here and now. However, there are global events taking place that have the potential to impact your business as we speak. Events that occur halfway around the world now affect Wall Street and Main Street on a daily basis; and like it or not, these events will continue to change the way business is conducted. Companies from Blockbuster, to small mom-and-pop cabinet shops in a garage all have the same challenge: to observe the transformations taking place in the world, and evolve in ways that ensure your prosperity from those changes.

Learn Before You Leap

My success as an adolescent entrepreneur was a double-edged sword. My parents begged me to go to college, but

I wouldn't hear of it. What was the point? I was convinced that I knew everything I needed to know in order to make money. I was, of course, clueless, and couldn't see the big picture. But as they say, hindsight is 20/20, and if I had to do things over again I would certainly have gone to college and learned everything I possibly could.

There are many large corporations that conduct business the same way I wanted to—as if they already know everything, which often becomes their Achilles heel. The fact that you are reading this book shows that you are hungry to learn new things. Bravo! Nothing is more important for your business success than knowledge; that is, if you then go out and apply what you've learned. It doesn't matter how responsible or self-reliant you are, or how hard you work. Unless you are constantly learning and broadening your horizons, you won't be equipped to make your best decisions. Considering the complexities of this century, it's never been more important to have a clear understanding of what's going on in the world and where you fit in. Bottom line: we are living in a time where knowledge is king.

> To exceed the expectations of others, we must first raise expectations of ourselves.

Curiosity Can Lead to Positive Change

Curiosity is one of the most important traits that an effective leader can possess. A great business leader should be reading everything he or she can get their hands on, as well as keeping a close eye on current events. Business leaders should be asking questions instead of just giving orders or advice, and listening to people outside their inner circle. When I was a teenager, I refused to listen to anyone throwing advice my way, but looking back I see that "you don't know what you're talking about" attitude was nothing more than arrogance. Many business leaders unfortunately behave that same way, as if they have all the answers, even if their companies are on (Federally supplied) life support.

Because of some horrendous past mistakes—both personal and professional—I eventually got some sense knocked into me and began to open up to other points of view. Over the years my curiosity about virtually everything has grown and proved invaluable in my efforts to move forward. Sometimes just one extra piece of information is all it takes to give my company a competitive edge. As the owner of Dark Horse Recording, I make it my business to know what other recording studios are up to, not only in Nashville, but all over the world. I often drop by other studios (there are still dozens of them in Nashville) to say hi. It never fails . . . their owners seem to enjoy telling me everything they're up to, what their take on the music industry is, and what their projections for the future are. The more questions I ask, the more they open up and the more I learn.

But what amazes me is that I've only had one recording studio owner come to me for a bit of advice in 16 years of operating this business. That one exception was a committee from a church (located across the country) that was installing a studio in their facility. They had the foresight to travel to Nashville and thoroughly research their options. The other studio owners in town don't seem to be the least bit curious as to how we've become so successful or how we've been able to continually expand at a time that so many other facilities have closed their doors. They don't seem to want to know what differentiates Dark Horse from their studios. There is one complex in Nashville that boasts eight recording studios, and is by far the biggest facility in this part of the country. The owner reportedly invested $27 million putting it all together and amassed an inventory of equipment that makes my head spin. His facility has recording consoles valued at $700,000. I have been to his company many times to get a bird's-eye view at what I'm up against; yet he has never once visited Dark Horse.

Curiosity is a quality that can—and should—be cultivated. Learning everything you can about your competitors and your customers can prove invaluable. That knowledge can make the difference in reeling in new clients, or adjusting your prices to maximize your bottom line. I encourage my staff and interns at Dark Horse to actively find out what's going on throughout the music industry. Show business is not unlike any other industry, and sustaining growth is more difficult than ever. The more curious you are and the more knowledgeable you become, the greater your chance to achieve success.

> *There can only be one solution to any problem: a change in attitude and in consciousness.*
>
> —Gregg Braden

A Business Model to Die For

Anyone who owns a laptop computer nowadays can record at a level of technical excellence that could be found only in a multimillion-dollar studio just 15 years ago. Therefore, the recording industry has become one of the world's worst business models. When I got into this field, the digital revolution was already changing everything; digital tape had just become the new gold standard. Even though new digital recording equipment was replacing older analog gear, you still needed the help of 400-pound digital tape machines and 10-foot mixing consoles in order to make great recordings. No one was predicting that almost overnight people would be able to record onto computer chips—thereby rendering many professional studios obsolete.

The first hard disk recording systems were quite pricey and unstable when they first came out, and didn't have the capacity to hold enough data for more than one song at time. Once again, no one was predicting that all that would change, and quickly. But change it did. Computer technology was evolving at the speed of light, and in the process affected virtually every corner of the business world. Dark Horse was into our sixth year when it became clear that the future of the studio industry was going to be brutal. This was my first business, and I had pushed every financial boundary imaginable in order to get the doors open. I was in debt up to my neck and there was no room for mistakes—I *had* to make this work. I had to evolve or die.

Our Challenge to Change

This technology explosion was the challenge to change at Dark Horse Recording. The digital revolution had made recording so affordable that artists, producers, and engineers were putting studios in their bonus rooms and walkout basements. Even some of the world's biggest stars were doing it—not so much to save money, but for the convenience and comfort of recording at home. Although some parts of the recording process—such as vocal and overdubs—could now be done in private homes, other aspects like recording drums, horns, strings, or choirs require a lot of square footage and much larger recording rooms. For instance, in order to record an orchestra, you might have to provide parking for 30 people, along with refreshments, bathrooms, and lounges. So we concentrated our efforts on finding ways to accommodate those situations. I began scratching my head asking myself, "What can I do to differentiate my facility and ensure that the people who *do* still use studios come to Dark Horse? What can I do to add value to each and every client who walks in the door?"

The most obvious thing that set us apart was the fact that Dark Horse was nestled in a country setting. Not only are we in a private and secluded environment with plenty of space to roam, but we sit on some of the most beautiful Tennessee hill country you've ever seen. It's absolutely gorgeous. In that sense, we are essentially a "guest ranch" that just happens to include a recording studio.

> Your success in any business will always be in direct proportion to your ability to *consistently exceed expectations* of your customers.

The prevailing mentality for studios is to buy more and more equipment in an effort to outdo the studio down the street. Dark Horse already had all the equipment to make great recordings as well as the track record to back it up. So instead of accumulating increasing amounts of recording equipment, I began adding kitchens, lounges, pavillions, observation decks, and so on. Rather than buying the latest "flavor of the month" microphone that no one really needed, I bought comfortable furniture. Instead of investing in the latest reverb device, I would invest in additional landscaping. All of these methods flew completely in the face of conventional studio wisdom. At one point, I even spent $35,000 on a 70-foot-wide stone entrance!

Our clients enjoyed and appreciated these amenities fully, and they accomplished two things. The amenities created a perception that Dark Horse was a five-star getaway normally reserved for the biggest recording stars, and they added to the value of my property.

It has become apparent to those of us at Dark Horse—as we continue to navigate our way into the twenty-first century—that our survival depends on creating an extraordinary customer experience for every client who walks through our door. We're constantly searching for creative ways to be more efficient while simultaneously doing whatever we can to add more value to our clients. In other words, it's our 100 percent commitment to evolve.

6 | The Alarm Is Sounding...and We Keep Hitting the Snooze Button

The problem with problems is that you can't solve a problem until you first recognize you have one. We are surrounded by all sorts of warning and alarm systems in everything from cell phones to our car's dashboard to make us aware of problems, and thus give us a chance to observe, react, and hopefully solve the problem. But many of the problems we face in business and in life don't come equipped with automatic alarm systems. Many of us have a generalized feeling of "unease" right now about life and business, but these storm clouds seem far off in the distance.

Wake-Up Call

Perhaps these ominous storms don't appear ominous enough just yet. But that doesn't mean those issues aren't deserving of your fullest attention. The alarm has gone off, but somebody keeps hitting the snooze button. We continue to fall back on the failed formulas of the past that are simply no longer effective. We continue the same dysfunctional habits . . . chasing after the same self-serving quests as we've always done. We don't seek to innovate or to reinvent, and we don't conserve or plan for a different future. Instead, we hop in our automobiles and drive endlessly to places we don't need to go, to buy items we don't really need to have. Our businesses and our families order stuff made in China, packed in Styrofoam, and shipped overnight so we get it the next morning. We drink from aluminum cans and then throw them into landfills. Restaurants serve water bottled in Italy, shipped to the United States for our pleasure. Unfortunately this kind of wastefulness has become the American way.

Today, more than 70 percent of the U.S. economy is consumer-based, meaning we simply buy stuff other people make. We've become a debtor nation in the meantime, borrowing money from other countries so we can buy stuff from other countries. This accounts for nearly three-fourths of the U.S. economy and that simply can't go on much longer. When that system fails (and it looks like it's doing that now), we've got to reinvent our business models to once again become a nation of producers rather than simply a collection of consumers.

Taken as a whole we have created a self-destructive culture and an unsustainable economy based on a senselessly ridiculous business model. Worse, we are doing nothing about it. Unlike China, India, and Japan, the United States doesn't really have a national economic policy or long-term economic goals—not really. The problem this situation causes for your business is that you are operating today in a business environment that can't be sustained and will not last. Therefore, you must begin now moving your company in the right direction. Eventually (and "eventually" may be sooner than you think) the economy will right itself and you'll be forced to comply with the new economic realities. Start now by figuring out where your company needs to be in the next 5 to 10 years and start moving in that direction now. It'll be easier and cheaper to move yourself than to wait for the coming economic tsunami to do it for you.

Sooner or later, I hope Americans will wake up to these new economic realities and put the country back on the right track. Seventy years ago we largely ignored the threats from Germany and Japan, but Pearl Harbor was a wake-up call. After that, we all got busy and eventually prevailed. But it was a very tough slog. An ounce of prevention could have paid huge dividends, but that's not how we as a nation tend to operate. What would the problems of illiteracy, obesity, and violence look like if we spent our resources on prevention instead of waiting until those resources must be spent on the result? We would save money, save lives, and put our country on track again. There's going to be an unthinkable price to pay if we don't quickly wake up to the countless warnings . . . the screaming alarm . . . and take action.

Just Who Is the Enemy?

All these gathering storms are terribly inconvenient, but the longer we delay dealing with them, the tougher it will be to adapt to or solve the problems they present. Issues like peak oil, global warming, and population growth don't carry the same punch as a sinister and diabolical enemy with a face, such as Osama bin Laden or Adolph Hitler. In World War II Americans were extremely motivated to do whatever was necessary to join together and sacrifice for the common good because they shared an enemy, which gave us a shared mission. Now we face an enemy that is not as diabolical or sinister at first glance. But make no mistake, these issues are an enemy as threatening as any in U.S. history. Because few people agree just what kind of enemy we're up against, it's easy to turn a blind eye. At the breakfast table on Saturday morning, December 6, 1941, you'd have heard many and varied opinions about the world situation and what the United States ought to do or not do. By the next morning, we had only one opinion and we *all* knew what we had to do.

Americans excel heroically at responding to crises such as 9/11, the Oklahoma City bombing, or the aftermath of Hurricane Katrina. In times of crisis, I've seen Americans rise to the occasion often putting their own safety on the back burner in order to help those in need. In moments like that, I find myself beaming with pride to be an American.

One would think that humans would be constantly evolving in an effort to make the world a better place. One would think it would be humanity's top priority to not only prosper, but to resolve conflicts in an effort to peacefully coexist on and with the planet. But, apparently this is not so. In the last century, more than 100 million people have died at the hands of each other, and we aren't treating the planet any better. As Pogo once remarked, "We have met the enemy, and he is us."

Perpetual Growth on a Finite Planet

Our entire world economic culture is based on expanding through constant growth, which is in direct conflict with surviving on a planet with finite resources. As the population grows and developing countries use more resources, the same pattern of growth that had brought a century of progress now threatens a dramatic reversal. To believe otherwise is to ignore the facts and physical limitations that are before us. We can't continue living on a planet with a finite resource base and fragile ecology while in a state of continual growth. It is simply not possible and not sustainable.

> *Where your talents and the needs of the world cross, lies your calling.*
> —Aristotle

Up until now, growing our economy has been based on the assumption that there will be a continual supply of energy and other natural resources. But in the coming years, it is inevitable that the cost of energy will continue to rise, the population will continue to expand, and our resources will continue to dwindle.

All developing nations are in relentless pursuit of economic growth and material goods, but when you extend this idea to its logical conclusion it's clear that we will soon hit a brick wall. We simply cannot return to business as usual after this current financial crisis that has put 15 million U.S. citizens out of work. It is not an option.

The alarm has gone off . . .

This is our wake-up call.

7 | The World Is on Fire

Remember the story of the frog and the bowl of water? If you place the frog in water that is already hot, the frog will immediately jump out; but if the water is cool—perhaps room temperature—and is *then* slowly heated, the frog will sink into a tranquil stupor, perhaps the way we might drift off in a hot bath. The frog will not perceive the danger as the water becomes hotter and hotter—because it happens slowly, by degrees. If someone doesn't help the poor frog out the water, it will be boiled to death.

We have collectively been behaving like that frog in recent years. We've somehow managed to ease ourselves into a warm bath of complacency—while seemingly unaware that the water around us is becoming hotter. In fact, things aren't just heating up: *the world's on fire!* And if we don't begin to change and take action, despite the obstacles that we are facing, we will suffer frog consequences.

Crisis Management

Many businesses are quick to react in a crisis. Most larger companies have a crisis management plan already in place. Reacting swiftly and effectively in a crisis is usually not the problem. Recognizing the business is facing a crisis, however, is much more difficult. If a "sea change" event happens suddenly, most everyone in the organization can see it. The crisis management plan is implemented and resources like money and people get allocated. Ad hoc teams are created to deal with "the crisis." The problem is when a crisis develops slowly. When that happens, most companies fail to recognize they are heading for a crisis (or are already in one). The time frame fools them into complacency. You simply cannot fix a problem if you don't recognize you have one, and most companies are reluctant to apply scarce resources to solving slowly developing problems. That's a big mistake. Problems are always much easier and cheaper to resolve when they are small. I've read several crisis plans from a variety of companies that outline in excruciating detail what actions the company will take if management discovers they are in "crisis mode," but I've never read a single one that covers identifying potential critical issues in advance and dealing with those problems early when they are small, more manageable, and cheaper to fix. It's all about reaction. Crisis management plans are there to *deal with* the crisis, not to identify when the company is headed toward one.

To accomplish what's never been accomplished, we must do what's never been done.

"Confirmation bias"

Business consulting faces similar issues. We tend to hire business consultants who will tell us what we want to hear. In fact, our prejudices are confirmed when the consultant tells us pretty much what we expected to learn. It is extremely rare for a business to hire a consultant or to seek business advice that goes against the grain of what management already thinks. But going against what is current conventional wisdom is exactly the prescription you need to be following today. And it's tough medicine to swallow, too.

"Confirmation bias" is a person's tendency to self-select or interpret new information in a way that backs up what they already believe. In other words, if you believe that global warming is a hoax, you will easily find circumstances that support your claim. Perhaps your hometown just had a record snowfall, so you say, "It doesn't look like global warming to me." Business falls prey to confirmation bias as easily as anyone. Crisis planning often conforms to our preconceived ideas about how crises develop. We hire consultants who tend to think like we do, and who tend to support and confirm what we already think and know. In business, not only do we often have "confirmation bias," we usually pay for it.

Every one of us is guilty of falling victim to this narrow-mindedness to some degree. Your confirmation bias will help support whatever stance you take on the environment, the economy, political views, religion, raising a family—or anything else under the sun. Most importantly, it allows us to go on our merry way, believing what we want to believe—whether it's true or not.

So we must choose to look at our businesses objectively and differently. We must choose to fight against complacency. We must choose to become better, more knowledgeable, more prepared. To overcome our obstacles and biases, we must simply look ahead.

I expect to pass through this world but once. Any good therefore that I can do, or any kindness that I can show to any fellow creature, let me do it now. Let me not defer or neglect it, for I shall not pass this way again.

—William Penn

Thinking Ahead

U.S. businesses are notorious for focusing only on *next* month's payroll, or completing the *next* project, or getting the *following* quarter's results. We continue to concentrate on the short term without giving any thought as to what the extended future holds. Of course, your business will fail if you can't make payroll; your boss will fire you if the project isn't completed; and your shareholders will have a fit if you don't hit your numbers. But in order to survive and prosper long term, we must design our businesses for the long term. We truly need to focus on the next several years, or even a decade ahead and not just next quarter.

But Americans don't do that very well, and that's been the problem. The issues we face—both as individual businesses and professionals and as a society at large—are in fact developing slowly. We have to focus on "now," because now *does* matter. But what happens next—after "now"? That deserves at least equal attention. We are acting more like the frog than we'd like to admit; and we all know what happened to the frog.

We have become a culture of instant gratification, and our businesses are a reflection of that culture. What's your business going to be like if employee health-care costs double, or oil hits $150 a barrel and stays there? When California won't allow your product to be sold in the nation's most populous state because of its packaging? When carbon taxes or environmental offsets are a line item in your budget? While those examples aren't upon us "now," they are indeed coming, and we need to focus some of our energy on what we're going to do about them. If we want business to get better we must begin thinking long term.

> *When you squeeze an orange, orange juice comes out—because that's what's inside. When you are squeezed, what comes out is what is inside.*
>
> —Wayne Dyer

The Price America Is Paying for Short-Term Thinking

U.S. commerce has fallen victim to poor health, and is now fighting a form of business cancer that reveals itself in the form of short-termism. As in physical cancer, some cells turn viciously against the body, and this is exactly what has happened with our "greed is good" mentality. Any time there is individual pursuit of selfish aims—short-term corporate goals taken to an extreme—we find ourselves in big trouble. Cheap hustlers, who exploit the weaker side of human nature, often accompany every business cycle, and fuel that type of short-term thinking. Pain and suffering follows, which unfortunately is the unpleasant medicine needed to bring about social and economic change. In our relentless pursuit of *more* without regard to the business ramifications, we've lost the better part of ourselves, as well as our notion of the core values upon which this country was built.

Our recent economic collapse has had a silver lining, as it's realigned our focus on family, financial security, and social outreach. Although it gives me no pleasure to make negative and potentially denigrating observations on U.S. society, it is my mission to light a fire under the apathy and complacency that got us here in the first place. When it comes to violence, education, health care, economic responsibility, and global warming, we should be taking the lead globally to set an example of leadership. All of these issues deserve our utmost attention. It's time for us to step forward and take action, because—as it's oft-quoted—with freedom comes responsibility.

Taking the Long View

There seems to be a direct connection between societies and cultures that take the long view and those who enjoy long-term survival. The Japanese are a fairly old society with roots that go back several thousand years. Compared to other modern nations, they tend to take the *long view* of economic problems. The British are long-view people as well, with an "Empire" that is nearly 1,000 years old. The Jewish people are another ancient culture—with more than 5,000 years of cultural heritage—all of them survivors who tend to think in the long term.

Americans, on the other hand, are the people of *now*. We are the instant gratification population who thrive on fast food, and work for companies whose idea of the future is the *"quarter after next."* The British may have invented microwaves, but we invented the *microwave oven*. U.S. consumers tend to buy products based on "what will it do for me *now*" rather than "how long will it last." If long-view cultures survive and instant gratification cultures perish, the United States is in for a hard future.

> A quarter is only 90 days. If you reported annually instead of quarterly, then you would make different discussions. If you expect to live longer than 90 days, then you should be focusing long term—*certainly* longer than a 90-day window. Focusing on the next quarter is only a good strategy if you're only going to live 90 days.

Companies that take the long view also prosper over those that only focus on the here and now. That means often foregoing immediate rewards in trade for long-term benefits. Legendary business figure Warren Buffett never came up with a really great ideas or invented anything; he simply invested for the long term in companies that shared his enduring thinking and avoided short-sighted organizations and investments. Short-term thinking might work, but it only works in the *short term*. Long-term thinking succeeds. We might not be short of oil today, but we know it's just a matter if time. We might not be able to tell exactly when we will run out of water, coal, natural gas, or forests, fish, and other natural resources, but the experts agree that there's a slow train coming and these resources will soon dwindle. The question is not *what* will happen—but when. Why should we only be concerned about a train bearing down on us at high speed? After all, does it really matter if you're hit by a fast train or a slow one? The goal should be to avoid getting run over at all.

> If we are not thinking long term, our businesses will be caught off guard and we'll end up responding only to crises. The threats we face offer an opportunity for every company to step up and begin integrating sustainable practices into the business models so that we create long-term profitability.

Each Day Is an Opportunity to Turn It All Around

The first step to turning our companies (and careers) around is for us to take responsibility for our part in allowing things to get so far out of control. We have become a culture of conspicuous consumption, with an unquenchable thirst for more. Collectively we have become a society where everybody feels that they are entitled, and deserving of having it all. Remember, it's our overindulgence and greed that caused the crash in the housing market, failing banks, a crumbling health-care system, climate change, and a dependency on foreign oil in the first place.

For your business to flourish in coming years, it will largely depend on your willingness to make changes in the way you run your business from today, going forward. And make no mistake, those business leaders who don't find ways to evolve will find their companies on the endangered list, threatened by the possibility of extinction.

8 | Our Civilization Is a Pyramid Scheme

We all basically know what a pyramid scheme is: an illicit money-making investment plan, or should I say trick, where early investors make out with profits paid for by the unsuspecting later investors. Eventually all such schemes always fail, and the losers are the ones who got in just a little too late and find themselves without a chair when the music stops.

Victim to Their Own Success

Ronald Wright, author of *Time Among the Maya,* said that "many civilizations rise because they find new ways to exploit every conceivable natural resource. Many civilizations feed on their local ecology until it is degraded, thriving only while they *grow*. When they can no longer *expand*, they fall victim to their own success. Does that remind you of anyone we know? Like *us*?! Our civilization is a pyramid scheme!

73

"*But*," you say, "Civilization produces products and services, art, architecture, science!" Well, then, perhaps you'd be
more comfortable comparing civilization to a multilevel marketing company, considered legal because it has *products*, but is
nonetheless "set up by design to blindly go past the saturation
point for membership and potential product sales and then . . .
keep on going, until it collapses under its own weight." When
my first book came out I was invited to speak at several Amway
meetings . . . the mother of all networking marketing meetings. Some of these audiences were five- or six-thousand strong,
great energy, wonderful people excited about solidifying their
financial independence and getting their share of the American
dream. But what they never realized is that their chances would
have been greater by going to Vegas and simply rolling the dice.
I soon learned that the only people making money were the
"Amway Diamond" promoters who rented out the hotels and
convention centers, raking in the ticket money under the guises
of training and education. That was Amway's dirty little secret.

A few years ago a friend of mine, *whom I had met at an
Amway meeting*, came to me with "gold fever" in his eyes telling
me about this new multilevel marketing company just getting
off the ground and how I could get in on the front end and
make out like a bandit. . . . And I fell for it, at least for a couple
of weeks, long enough to attend one of their initial meetings.
This time around the scheme didn't last a year before it came
crashing down.

Of course, the pyramid scheme is not new. The archaeologi-
cal record shows that Mayan civilization lasted about 1,500 years
and mastered remarkable levels of mathematical, astronomical,
and architectural skills not to mention developing their own
written language. So, of course, it prospered and expanded for

1,400 years, but then, in the last 100 years before collapse, chose to profligately expend its people and resources on *real* pyramids. To build them, the population expanded even as their natural resources were depleted and much of the best land was paved over in building cities. All of that development fell on the backs of slaves and artisan classes, and while the lucky few at the top of the society grew fat and enjoyed the spectacle of human sacrifice, those at the malnourished bottom literally became stunted in their growth and were quite *literally* at risk of *being* sacrificed to the Mayan pyramid scheme.

Can history repeat itself? In this age of knowledge and awareness, we've certainly learned from our mistakes, right? Apparently not. Currently (as 2010 gets under way), the world population is an estimated 6.8 billion. Since births outnumber deaths, the world's population is expected to reach about 9 billion by the year 2040. That is, of course, barring nuclear war, a return of the Black Plague, a deadly flu epidemic, or the collapse of our food production infrastructures leading to massive starvation.

History's Biggest Ponzi Scheme

In 2008, the Bernie Madoff scandal showed that even investors presumed to be sophisticated can be tricked into joining a Ponzi scheme by a promoter with a good story. When people catch wind of the possibility of easy money, they hear what they want to hear. This is not a new idea. One would think that experienced individuals would know better than to invest in something that sounds too good to be true.

Falling for stories that are too good to be true is exactly what we've been doing when it comes to recognizing economic and

environmental crises. The facts are in and the signs are everywhere. Too many people continue to listen to too many stories
about how all this will work out fine in the end even if we do
nothing about it. It should be obvious to everyone that we live
on a finite planet with finite resources, and, therefore, we should
act accordingly. As the population continues to grow at an exponential rate and *all* natural resources are peaking or diminishing,
something's got to give. But we have a conflicting belief that
perpetual growth is necessary to keep the world spinning and
the global economy chugging along. In essence, we're operating
in a worldwide Ponzi scheme of sorts. We're borrowing from
our children's energy and environmental future so that we can
selfishly realize short-term benefits today.

Outside of the ever-present profit motive, Americans have
generally been well intentioned, wanting to share our high living
standard and democratic processes with the rest of the planet.
But in doing so, we've sometimes set a bad example for the rest
of the world.

As we have climbed the ladder of success and encouraged
others to follow, we have been kicking out the rungs below us.
Where once we had small communities with local, sustainable
agriculture and small businesses, we now have huge cities de-
pendent on food from far-flung sources even as we pursue global
business models and outsourced labor. Since we *want* the party
to go on forever, we will have to be *forced* to conserve, to develop
sustainable models, to police and regulate where we might have
preferred a *laissez faire* approach. If we do not find ways to more
rationally share the earth's bounty, then we will all find ourselves
in a far worse place than Bernard Madoff's investors, because the
engine of progress has no reverse gear, no FDIC, and no Federal
Reserve to bail us out. When we look at the depth and scope of

the situation, Madoff is a small-time offender compared to the monumental Ponzi scheme we're all engaged in.

We've been running up an ecological tab as if there's no tomorrow. That's okay, as long as there is no tomorrow.

Do you know that in the United States we waste 50 percent of our food? I was speaking at a hotel a few weeks ago, and in one of the restaurants they had a lunch buffet with so much food displayed I felt that I owed the gluttonous Romans an apology. People were eating so much they could hardly stand up and walk out the door. By the time I arrived it was almost time to close down the food service, but yet they kept bringing the food out to make it appear that even the last person would be creating their meal from a full, unspoiled banquet. In the United States, we don't know the meaning of enough. Never mind that more than a billion people go to bed hungry every night or that 30,000 children under the age of five die every single day of malnutrition. We'll just let our kids deal with the consequences of our little pyramid scheme. Don't worry 'cause we bought in . . . in the nick of time. Or did we?

During the twentieth century alone, world population multiplied by a factor of four, while our consumption grew by 40 times. That doesn't seem to match up, does it? And unfortunately, the pyramid scheme we're now running involves *everyone*. Once upon a time the collapse of a society was a local or regional phenomenon, but with globalization there is no haven. We are exploiting *all* of the rain forests, fresh water, coral reefs, fish, wildlife, oil, and minerals *everywhere*.

And what are we building with those resources? Basically, more pyramids: cities, jumbo jets, Humvees, plasma screens, and enough nonbiodegradable waste to last until our sun explodes. And while Wall Street engages in excesses fit for those long-dead Mayan kings, we watch our resources being depleted even as the disenfranchised literally starve. Consider that the number of people in the world presently living in abject poverty is now equal to the *entire* world population in 1900. And this is happening, according to United Nations figures, while the world's three richest *individuals* have a net worth equal to that of the poorest 48 *countries*.

But a pyramid scheme is so attractive precisely because it sells hope and promises wealth and independence to all. Unfortunately, we've reached saturation and are running out of things to sell to an increasingly impoverished clientele. And I, for one, am no longer buying.

It's time, no, long *past* time for our leaders to do more than offer promises and panaceas. Or perhaps it's time we get personal. It's time each and every one of us steps up with personal leadership. We must think farther ahead than this weekend. It's time we stop spending our children's inheritance. We must become like the man who plants trees under which he will never sit. We must develop a culture of shared sacrifice. Whether we like it or not, the party's over.

When is the last time you did the math . . . our population will grow by another 50 percent in just 40 years, yet all of our natural resources have already peaked. These are not opinions, they're facts. I'm not an alarmist and I don't have a string of environmental degrees. I'm simply a concerned citizen.

There is neither time nor room left to maneuver. We can no longer just "keep on going." We all, especially our leaders worldwide, must act to limit our numbers and our environmental impact. If we do not replace our pyramid scheme mentality with a fair and sustainable sharing of what the earth offers, then we, like the Maya, are headed for a collapse that will make the Dark Ages enviable.

All Our Challenges Are Interconnected

Several years ago I had the privilege of attending one of the Carter Foundation's "Board of Councilors" meetings in Atlanta. A half-hour before the meeting started, President and Mrs. Carter entered the foyer where breakfast treats were being served and proceeded to greet everyone and engage in light conversation. Once assembled in the auditorium we heard several speakers report on their efforts to eradicate Guinea Worm disease, which causes river blindness... one of the Carter Foundations commitments. I was inspired by the sense of compassion and hope as I listened to reports on their progress and on going challenges. Then President Carter took the stand and proceeded to speak for about 15 minutes before closing out the meeting. I couldn't help but be impressed with how sharp his observations were, and how informed he was on current issues. He finished by saying "I'll take a couple of questions before we dismiss."

This was my chance to interact. For several years I had been researching global warming and my head was full of questions about climate change. I knew this issue was important to President Carter... after all, he was the man who had 32 solar panels installed on the roof of the White House during his term in office. Although the panels were removed soon after Ronald

Reagan moved in, in an attempt to assure U.S. citizens that such drastic actions would no longer be necessary.

After answering two questions, one about the Guinea Worm disease and one about resolving conflict in the Middle East, the President announced there was time for one more question. So in a room of 300 people I stood up and raised my hand, and he made eye contact and motioned for me to speak. "Mr. President, as climate change intensifies, do you think third-world countries, which are already water stressed and unstable, will break out in conflict and ultimately war over food and water?" He looked me straight in the eye and for the next five minutes proceeded to lay out how volatile, toxic, and unstable things are in some of the world's poorest countries. He said there is little doubt that there will be violence and uprisings associated with climate change, and it will only get worse if global warming is not somehow subsided. He reminded everyone in the room that more than 1 billion people on the planet still live on less than one dollar a day and we need to come together, as countries, as regions, as world citizens, to address these collective problems. In no uncertain terms he viewed global warming as a military threat.

President Carter's reply to my question put me on a quest to learn more about just how interconnected all these global issues are and what's likely to happen if we don't solve them and soon. Not only are the problems we face interconnected, but the solutions are interconnected as well.

How Will This Affect You?

Climate change and the other before mentioned global issues have already begun to affect your business in small ways today, and over time these issues will intensify, and the ripple effect will continue to impact your business more and more. You can start preparing by making small incremental changes now, while they are easy and relatively cheap rather than waiting them out and trying to make fast changes that are inherently risky and expensive. In business, good management manages risk, and it is risky not to begin addressing these issues now.

You are the way you are because that's the way you want to be. If you really wanted to be any different, you would be in the process of changing right now.

—Fred Smith

9 | Five Bright Lights

The individuals, companies, and concepts that are spotlighted in this chapter are shining examples demonstrating how we can evolve and move forward toward a more prosperous future. We can do this! We can awaken the giant that lies sleeping in each one of us, and step up to the challenges before us. The following are some wonderful illustrations of the American spirit in action, and that spirit is alive and well. In this chapter I spotlight some individuals and companies who are busy coming up with innovative ways to do business. These entrepreneurial minds, or forward thinkers if you will, are doing great work as business owners and community leaders. Most importantly, you will see that what's good for business is also good for the planet.

> *What lies behind us, and what lies before us, are tiny matters compared to what lies within us.*
>
> —Ralph Waldo Emerson

Recession Gardens

In my Seven Step Challenge (later in this book) I'll be talking about the philosophy of shared sacrifice, and sharing how millions of Americans planted "victory gardens" during World War II as a way to save money. A staggering 40 percent of all our country's vegetables were being grown in people's home gardens during that war. Sixty-five years later as U.S. families are facing the highest unemployment rate since the great depression, once again many are turning to their backyards, rather than the grocery store, as a source for produce. With the pressures that people are feeling, the phrase "evolve or die" is resonating in the back of people's minds and Americans are finding new ways to be more resourceful. So citizens are taking this positive example from our past, and are planting what are now called "recession gardens." The National Gardening Association estimates that 43 million U.S. households are now growing their own vegetables, fruits, and herbs. Eating healthier at an affordable price makes all the sense in the world. A family will get an average 25-to-1 return on its investment in a garden. That means that a household spending $200 on a medium-to-large garden can save as much as $5,000 in grocery bills over the course of a year. This is a great example of turning crisis and change into opportunity, because many people are discovering that growing your own food has advantages well beyond saving money.

Four Great Reasons to Grow Your Own Garden

1. Homegrown produce simply tastes better. If you care deeply how your food tastes, then it makes sense that an tomato grown by a local farmer and never refrigerated will retain more of its flavor than if it's crated, refrigerated, and jostled for thousands of miles from Mexico.
2. Growing your own is healthier. You can grow organically and avoid using pesticides and antibiotics, and by growing in richer soil you get more nutritional value.

3. Growing your own food is safe. By growing it yourself you eliminate all the steps between your food's source and your table, thereby dramatically reducing the chance of contamination or disease.
4. Growing locally promotes community. Many people are growing gardens in co-op fashion, and the whole process becomes a social event.

> Being adaptable to change is the most important factor to success.

Miel Bistro

Restaurants have also gotten in on the act of reinvigorating their menus while saving money in the process. Restaurant managers are planting their own gardens on rooftops, in the back lot, or even right in the midst of their dining patios. They have done this not only to save money, but also to provide better and fresher products to their customers.

Jimmy Phillips and Seema Prasad, owners of Miel Bistro in Nashville, have taken the idea of a recession garden, turned it on its head, and incorporated the concept as a major part of their business plan. In 2008, in the midst of $4 a gallon gasoline and an economy in free-fall, they were ready to pull the trigger on their lifelong dream, the opening of a high-end, yet approachable and sustainable, neighborhood eatery. Despite the perfect storm of obstacles they faced at opening time, they were determined to proceed as planned with the opening of Miel. And that's just what they did.

For Jimmy and Seema, starting a recession garden on a small scale simply wouldn't do. Their business plan included the following commitments:

- Starting their own small "urban" farm, 10 minutes from the restaurant, which provides a substantial amount of the produce used on their menu.
- Creating additional local jobs on this farm, which as it expands will create more jobs, and eventually supply locally grown, organic produce to other small local restaurants.
- Showing that Miel Bistro supports their community's economy by using locally produced meats, honey, and dairy products.
- Recycling and composting.

In business models of the past, management concentrated strictly on the financial bottom line, but moving forward management must also consider the impact of their company's actions on society and the environment. This is the definition of "double-bottom line," and this way of thinking, followed by corresponding actions, have allowed Jimmy and Seema to authentically brand Miel as a community contributor and innovator—which helps attract customers.

The restaurant business, even in the best of times is challenging. Having virtually no advertising budget, differentiating themselves on day one from the competition was crucial for Miel. By following their convictions, Jimmy and Seema succeeded in creating consistent local buzz in the media, on which a price tag cannot be placed. They have not just ridden the economic storm out, they are thriving. Every week new guests walk in their doors, and walk out raving fans. And just think, the seeds of their success, were planted, quite literally . . . in a garden. By the way, in case you are curious, Miel means honey in French and Spanish.

Whether it's your family or a locally owned restaurant that's growing these gardens, another added benefit is that you are lowering your carbon footprint. Growing locally cuts out the need to transport those fruits and vegetables sometimes thousands of miles. It's healthier for you and healthier for the planet. This is a prime example of how the solution to becoming more efficient and saving money is also the same solution to saving the environment.

Great ideas often receive violent opposition from mediocre minds.
—Albert Einstein

Hard Rock Cafe

The Hard Rock Cafe has 127 locations worldwide and yet again the restaurant is trying out a forward-thinking idea . . . actually a "Pay-It-Forward" idea. Even though we're in the midst of the worst economic downturn in half a century, Hard Rock's Nashville location with Jim McGonagle as the general manager has been doing quite well. But they hadn't remodeled since they opened in 1994 and were long overdue for a change. So they closed their doors for three months to renovate and expand their space by nearly double. Besides expanding their seating capacity, they will also be adding new memorabilia, which will include a suit from Hank Williams Jr. and shoes from Michael Jackson.

In correlation with their motto "Love All, Serve All," all 71 of their employees will be retained on the payroll during the three months of downtime at the restaurant, and will be paid to do community service. This is an idea that wins in all directions. In one fell swoop, Jim and the Hard Rock Cafe have accomplished a number of positive outcomes:

1. Local nonprofits are thrilled to have the extra help, and these acts of service will surely spread goodwill throughout the community.
2. The Hard Rock Cafe has just empowered their 71 employees in the art of "paying it forward." These employees will help in soup kitchens, thrift stores, and beyond as volunteers, while still getting paid.
3. The Hard Rock Cafe has branded their image of a trusted community partner into the minds of business and city leaders throughout the region, confirming the perception of a company willing to put their money where their mouth is with their motto, "Love All, Serve All." This will pay dividends for years to come, and inspire other business leaders to think in similar patterns.
4. This gesture will no doubt inspire other businesses and corporations to follow suit with donations of volunteer time.
5. The Hard Rock Cafe retains its greatest asset—it's people. They will *not* have to reinvest in interviewing, hiring, and training new employees, and that's a real cost savings.

Would I be going too far to say this is a cutting-edge business philosophy? You decide. The best part is in the knowing that the ripple effects of the Hard Rock reaching out beyond their own four walls simply can't be measured. When they reopen, I for one plan to make the 30-minute pilgrimage to downtown Nashville and support the Hard Rock Café for stepping up and ultimately making a difference in the lives of others.

Ideas are the mightiest influence on earth. One great thought breathed into a man may regenerate him.

—William Ellery Channing

UPS

When is the last time you saw a UPS truck making a left turn? I'm willing to guess you haven't, and that's because UPS trucks have been using the strategy of making only right turns for decades. Their drivers have a no-left-turn rule. It's just one of the techniques that UPS uses to speed up delivery times and to be more fuel-efficient. Years ago, their managers used to plot on maps how those trucks could be efficiently driven turning mostly right. (Think about how long you have to wait to make a left turn at most intersections.) Now they have computers and sophisticated programming that allows them to plot out right-turn routes.

But do you know just how much their no-left-turn rule saves? Annually, UPS trucks drive 2.5 billion miles, and that one idea saves them 28.5 million miles of wear and tear on their trucks, and 3 million gallons of fuel each year alone! This is a prime example of thinking in terms of how efficiency can lead to greater profitability. And as an added bonus, UPS employees tend to take the philosophy home into their personal driving habits as well. UPS personifies a mammoth company that is rethinking the way they do business in the twenty-first century.

> *A little more persistence, a little more effort, and what seemed hopeless failure may turn to glorious success.*
> —Elbert Hubbard

Walmart

Every time I visit a Walmart I'm reminded how much influence that organization has. They're . . . sooooo . . . huge! So when I learned of the depth of their commitment to lowering their carbon footprint, I was thrilled. In recent years, Walmart has been making some truly remarkable changes for the greater good, as they have unveiled plans to boost energy efficiency and cut down on waste in an effort to reduce greenhouse gases. They are pursuing every imaginable avenue to be more efficient. The company is currently working to cut energy usage at its stores by 30 percent. With a company this large (they employ 1.8 million people), making small changes can make a *big* difference. For instance, improving fuel mileage in the trucking fleet by 1 mile per gallon would save more than $52 million per year. They have pledged to eliminate a quarter of the solid waste used by their U.S. stores and warehouses through reduced packaging.

Walmart understands that if they throw something away, they must pay to haul it away. That means they had to buy it first, which means they end up paying for it twice. They realize that being one of the largest companies in the world means environmental problems are their problems. Bottom line is that these changes boil down to good business. The payback on their pledge saves millions of gallons of fuel, millions of trees, and millions of dollars. Also, they have developed an entire web site dedicated to helping their customers become more green-friendly with their buying decisions.

All these businesses have one thing in common: they are companies that are *evolving*. They haven't stopped in their quest to find better ways to do business, thereby keeping their competitive edge. They are creating new ways to adapt to the constant change the twenty-first century is presenting. Most importantly, these companies are doing what it takes to step up to the challenges that are before us.

PART II

Seven-Step Challenge

Throughout this book, I've written about lessons that I've learned from a lifetime as an entrepreneur and business owner. It's from those experiences that I have created my *Seven-Step Challenge*. As you read about each of these steps, let the ideas, concepts, and strategies serve as a critical resource for you to take your organization to the next level. Time and time again I've witnessed companies that were forced to close their doors because they refused to change with the times. They allowed obstacles and adversities to pull them under, instead of viewing those challenges as opportunities to evolve.

My Seven-Step Challenge is designed to serve as a road map for getting your business from where it is to where you want it to be. Some steps you've no doubt heard before—for instance, *exceeding expectations*—but I believe they are so fundamentally important it's worth putting them back in the spotlight. Although you might feel that you've heard that phrase one too many times, the truth is that there's no better strategy for getting noticed by your customers, competitors, or boss. In fact, some of the most successful CEOs and entrepreneurs of all time have used

93

the strategy of exceeding expectations to differentiate themselves from the pack. Some of my other steps—like multidimensional thinking, or triple bottom line business philosophy—will likely be new to you. Though unfamiliar, these ideas might pull you right out of your comfort zone—which just might be the push you need to move your businesses forward.

The ways in which we conduct business are changing faster with each passing day, and as the pace of our world continues to accelerate, so will those changes. Those who adapt best will be the most successful in every area of the business world. My goal is for these seven steps to inspire you to take more risks and look at your company in new ways and from new perspectives. Whether you are working in a large corporation or contemplating your first business start-up, consider how this challenge can become a powerful tool for you to gain and maintain the competitive edge.

Step 1:
Do Whatever
It Takes to
Exceed
Expectations

It never ceases to amaze me that companies spend millions to attract new customers (people they don't know) and spend next to nothing to keep the ones they've got! Seems to me the budgets should be reversed!

—Tom Peters

Standing Out at GE

No one would have ever guessed that when famed corporate leader Jack Welch began his career with General Electric, he would eventually become the most successful chairman and CEO in the company's history. During Welch's reign, GE's market capitalization increased by a staggering $400 billion— making it the most valuable corporation in history. Jack Welch reinvented, restructured, and revolutionized GE, and created the gold standard by which all other CEOs are measured.

One of Welch's first projects was developing a new type of plastic called polyphenylene oxide for industrial use. He adopted a personal strategy from the beginning to "exceed expectations and stand out from the crowd" by always going the extra mile. And he clearly *did* get himself noticed when, in 1968, he was promoted to general manager of the entire plastics division. He was only 32 years old, and GE's youngest general manager.

Exceeding expectations is a strategy that can apply to anyone in any position at any company. Sometimes the simplest of concepts are the most powerful and profound. There's no better or faster method for getting noticed and standing out to your external and internal customers.

There is real magic in enthusiasm. It spells the difference between mediocrity and accomplishment.

—Norman Vincent Peale

Traveling Car Wash

I recently decided to have my car washed and detailed, and needed to find someone who specialized in "on-site professional auto detailing"; in other words, someone who could travel out to Dark Horse to do the job so I could stay focused on other things. So I opened the Yellow Pages and stumbled on a couple of guys who promised to come over that day. This was my first experience with traveling car-wash entrepreneurs, so I wasn't sure what to expect.

That afternoon, two unshaven, scruffy young men pulled up, introduced themselves, and announced that they were ready to work. Although they didn't strike me as the kind of people who would pay close attention to detail (no pun intended), when they opened the doors to their aging, dented, rusted out van, I was surprised to find it fully equipped. There was a huge tank of water—big enough to swim in—a pressure washer, and a comprehensive assortment of tools and cleaning products. They even had their own generator that provided them with electricity for their vacuum and polishing tools. Not only were they professional and thorough, but they went the extra mile in every respect, cleaning every microscopic nook and cranny, inside and out. There are few things more exciting than when someone exceeds your expectations. My car hadn't looked that good since the day I bought it. I was thrilled!

Within the next 24 hours, I found myself turning my friends on to these two car-washing entrepreneurs. Their operation might be small, but there are dozens of large companies who could learn a thing or two from these two rugged entrepreneurs. When you exceed your customer's expectations, they become raving fans, and therefore the most important part of your recruiting team.

> *Your most unhappy customers are your greatest source of learning.*
> —Bill Gates

The Fall of Circuit City

Author Jim Collins cites electronic retail chain Circuit City in his bestselling book *Good to Great* as one of 11 companies that made the difficult jump to greatness. As Collins explains, "Circuit City saw that it could become 'the McDonald's' of big-ticket retailing, able to operate a geographically dispersed system by remote control." I'm not sure what all that means, but it was no surprise to me when Circuit City filed for bankruptcy in 2009 and shut down its remaining 567 stores—putting 34,000 people out of work. Sorry Jim, but it would now appear that Circuit City has gone from *good to bankrupt*.

For years, Circuit City had been the go-to place for my children and me to buy movies, DVD players, stereos, and other electronic gear. They had a perfect location 10 minutes from our home, next to a grocery store, movie theater, and, most importantly, next to my favorite bookstore. However, I had become increasingly frustrated with their total lack of customer service. There comes a point where convenience gets trumped by the need for a better in-store experience. And no matter how big a company is, their success boils down to the sum total of individual customer experiences. Though Circuit City blamed its closure on "unprecedented pullback in consumer spending," I would venture to guess that wasn't the *whole* story. I can recall three separate occasions during the year prior to the store's demise when I attempted to buy products from them—and became so weary standing in line that I set down my purchase and walked out the door. Just think about it. They had customers who were trying *to spend money*-the Crow family-yet they made the process as difficult as possible.

Why? During "light" shopping hours they had closed down the normal cash registers and directed the revenue-generating customers to the "service register." Yet there was never a time that I didn't see plenty of employees wandering throughout the store. Have you ever stood in line at a service register? Inevitably those at the front of the line are engaged in lengthy debates about returning, exchanging, or repairing previously purchased items. In other words, it can take *forever*.

The amount of time, energy, and money that businesses such as Circuit City use for advertising in order to lure a customer in the door—only to have them essentially ignored when they get there—simply amazes me. Imagine a customer making it all the way into the store, selecting their purchase—then actively choosing not to buy it because of a policy blunder or plain lack of in-store leadership? It seems to me that people tend to forget that customers are a company's only source of revenues. I'd be willing to bet Circuit City's demise had less to do with a pullback in customer spending and everything to do with the way they failed to empower their employees to take care of their most precious resource: their customers.

> If you own the problem, you own the customer.
> If you lose the problem, you lose the customer.

Attention to Detail

My son Joseph's attention to detail—combined with his passion for preparing food—has resulted in an impressive career at a young age. Yet to this day, I still haven't been able to figure out what ignited his zeal for fine cuisine. It was as if Joseph's enthusiasm for the culinary arts was in his DNA from birth. He's been in the kitchen experimenting with whatever leftovers or random staples he could find in the cupboard since his early teens. It was always a treat merely to watch him fix an after-school snack, flipping knives and spatulas as he prepared his feast. Every plate of food was a work of art; watching him slice and carve a piece of fruit was mesmerizing. When other kids his age were watching TV, Joseph was soaking up culinary magazines such as *Saveur* and *Gourmet* and reading books like *The Soul of a Chef* and *Kitchen Confidential*.

Then at the age of 15, Joseph landed a summer job as a busboy at Antonio's, an authentic Italian restaurant just a few miles from our home. He went from washing dishes and busing tables to making salads and desserts in no time. The owners couldn't help but notice how well he paid attention to every detail, whether he was meeting with suppliers or making authentic Italian sauces. By the time he was 17, he had worked his way up from first course/cold station cook, to grill cook, to sous-chef. Joseph always took pride preparing each culinary presentation with great attention to the smallest detail.

Now in his mid-twenties, Joseph is the executive chef at Rumba, a popular Nashville Asian-fusion restaurant, where he is responsible for creating the daily specials and managing the kitchen. With his single-minded focus and extreme attention to detail, Joseph has become a world-class chef in every sense of the word. He knows that paying great attention to detail will exceed your customers' expectations every time.

The thing that keeps a business ahead of the competition is excellence in execution.

—Tom Peters

A Tale of Two Singers

It was April 1997 when I received a call from a producer, Scott Hendricks, who was in the midst of producing country singer

Faith Hill's second CD. They needed to change studios, and Scott was ready to give my new studio Dark Horse Recording a try.

As you might imagine, I was thrilled. Back then, my fledgling business was in its infancy. Dark Horse Recording was little more than a home studio attached to my log house on my newly purchased 10-acre farm; a far cry from the 24-hour-a-day, four-studio complex that it's now become. I'd be willing to bet that if Faith Hill was coming to your home every day for five weeks, you'd be highly inspired to keep her happy. And for good reason: Faith will tell you that a lot more goes into creating a hit record than meets the eye. For instance, for every day she would sing, Scott would spend another day by himself, editing her best vocal performances together to create an even more extraordinary vocal performance. This is the way most records are made, and that extreme pursuit of excellence is one of the reasons Faith Hill has sold more than 40 million records and accumulated 8 number-one singles and 3 number-one albums.

On their first Saturday at Dark Horse, Scott was in the studio by himself editing vocals. I decided to fix him one of my "*almost famous*" deli sandwiches. I wish you could taste one—freshly baked bread, four different kinds of lunch meats, Swiss and cheddar cheese, and red ripe tomatoes. More importantly, I wish you could have heard Scott's compliments all afternoon. I started thinking... "he's been here at Dark Horse for a week and hasn't said one thing about the studio, whether he liked the acoustics, what he thought of my choice of equipment or the way the piano sounds—but he continued raving about that sandwich for the rest of the afternoon. It was obvious that I had struck a chord. So that night, I stocked the studio refrigerator with every conceivable ingredient to make every deli sandwich imaginable. Then I began fixing them for Faith and Scott every day, and would often join them in a shaded picnic area right outside the studio.

This went on for about a month, until one day they came to me saying that they were running behind schedule, and asked if I had two more weeks of studio time available. I must have had a lot of nerve, because I responded—in a moment of cockiness—"Well, it just so happens that we have exactly two weeks open until Neil Diamond begins recording for the rest of the summer. And I know that you're in the middle of your stay here, but I've decided to raise my studio rates by $75 a day going forward. Would you have any problem with that price increase?" For a minute there was an awkward silence in the air; after all, I had put everyone on the spot. Before Scott had time to respond, Faith chimed in and said, "I don't have a problem with that Robin. The sandwiches alone are worth it!"

Faith's comment about my sandwiches triggered an *ah-ha* moment in which I realized two things that would shape the future of Dark Horse Recording. One: All this time I had been thinking that I was in the business of "high tech equipment," perfectly calibrated flying fader systems, acoustically correct listening environments, flawless grounding systems, and so on. However, I quickly realized that I'm truly in the *people* business; that my studio's high-tech wizardry is merely a vehicle for serving *people*. Two: Exceeding customer expectations would become my secret weapon to gaining the competitive edge.

> *I slept and dreamt that life was joy*
> *I awoke and saw that life was service*
> *I acted and behold service was joy*
> —Rabindranath Tagore (Bengali poet of Calcutta)

Since that time I've fixed carrot juice for Wynonna Judd, hamburgers for Amy Grant, barbeque chicken for Michael McDonald, and shish kebabs for Neil Diamond. You might be wondering—does Robin do anything for his clients besides feeding them? There are countless other things we've come up with to creatively service our customers, at little or no expense (besides fixing food), that I will share with you shortly.

You might also be thinking, "Big deal, Robin. Anyone would enjoy fixing sandwiches for Faith Hill!" I admit, you've got a good point. But everyone who works at Dark Horse knows that all of our clients have fundamentally the same needs—whether they are famous or not. Since opening our doors for business, we've continued to grow with a commitment to give each client the best possible recording experience. I've learned a profound life lesson: exceed the expectations of your clients, and they'll become the ambassadors for your company—which is absolutely priceless.

The secret of getting ahead is getting started!

—Agatha Christie

Tim McGraw on Fire

The second half of my tale serves as an amusing bookend to my deli sandwich experience, as it involves another country artist who Faith knows quite well; her husband, Tim McGraw.

Recently, Tim came to Dark Horse for an extended stay to record his *Southern Voice* CD. In many ways, his was one of the most challenging productions to ever come our way. Tim's group—which included his producer, band, crew, private chefs, and engineers—rented all four of our studios, our two apartments, and guest house. Because there were more people than beds available, they also brought in a 45-foot tour bus equipped with 12 bunks and a double bed in the rear—and parked it right outside one of the studios. Although all of them live in the Nashville area, the entire entourage—including Tim himself—slept right here on the property, thereby completely immersing themselves in the creative process.

Tim had recorded his two previous albums at an elegant but remote studio facility high in New York's Catskill Mountains, so coming to Dark Horse was his way of having the best of both worlds. On one hand he was free from distraction; he was able to sequester himself on the property as if he was recording in some faraway location. Yet he was also close enough to go home to be with his family from time to time.

> Creating an extraordinary experience for your clients should be your *top priority*.

As the sun went down on their first day of recording, I was out on the grounds by a large stone fire pit warming my hands over a fire I had just started. Then I looked up only to see Tim heading toward me with an armload of logs which he proceeded to dump onto the fire and then return to the log pile for yet another load. Pretty soon, the two of us had made a half dozen trips carrying wood and building up the fire to epic proportions. As we began to engage in some friendly conversation I found myself asking him all kinds of questions. When I inquired about his children, he told me how he loved coaching his daughter's basketball team. When I asked where he went to school, he began reminiscing about his love for playing on the high school football team. And when I asked about his family, he lit up as he told me the story of when he was just 13 years old watching his father, Tug McGraw, pitch the final strike to give the Philadelphia Phillies their first World Series Championship. It seemed everything we discussed continued to lead us back to his love of sports, especially football.

As the week went on I kept thinking back on our conversation, brainstorming with myself on things we might do to enhance his experience here at Dark Horse. When the following Monday rolled around, I asked my staff to pull the projector from our media room and place it outdoors atop a scaffold. We then created a 14-foot projection screen out of lighting stands with a huge white drop cloth, and assembled a small concert PA system we had in storage. After a few hours spent getting everything in place, we had assembled an outdoor movie theater.

That night it was a sight to see . . . Tim, his band, and crew all seated around the blazing bonfire eating barbeque as they watched Monday night football in high definition—with the sound booming out almost as if they were right there in the stadium. *They loved it!* Every time I ran into Tim that week, he would say, "Hey Robin, we're going to do that Monday night football thing again next week, right?" So that's exactly what we did. For the next two months, we converted our picnic area into the "Dark Horse Outdoor Movie Theater" every Monday night.

Without spending a single extra dollar, we found a way to design an unanticipated and exceptional experience for Tim and his entourage. When Tim recalls his experience here several years from now, he's probably not going to remember what kind of microphones or recording consoles we had or what kind of furniture we had in the lounge. His most powerful memory will be hanging out with the people he cares about, kicking back a couple of beers, and enjoying his Monday night football—like the regular guy he is.

Orville Wright did not have a pilot's license.
—Gordon McKenzie

The Dark Horse Driving Range

Dark Horse's biggest client during our first year in business was producer Steven V. Taylor, who recorded close to 100 days at my studio in our first year. When he wasn't on sight producing, he was likely to be found playing a few rounds of golf at one of several courses in the area. He absolutely loved the game. It just so happened that I had a 4-acre horse pasture on my property that I thought might serve as a nice driving range. So I fired up our tractor/lawnmower, and over the following month, I continued mowing the grass shorter and shorter. It was spring, so the grass was easy to train. The field soon began to take shape, so I went out and bought a bucket of golf balls, a few golf clubs. Voilà—the new "Dark Horse Driving Range" was ready for action!

These ideas didn't require a PhD to create, and needed little to no investment to execute. No matter what kind of business you're in, no matter how big or small your enterprise is, you can find countless ways to exceed expectations for your customers with a little creativity and imagination.

All our clients fundamentally have the same needs, whether they are famous or not. They want a great recording experience—complete with a few touches of home, or their favorite pastime/food/sport. In the 16 years since Dark Horse opened, we've continued to grow and hone our commitment to going above and beyond the expectations of each and every client who walks in our door.

I never would have imagined when starting my company that we would be building an outdoor theater or creating a driving range as a strategy to gain the competitive edge in the studio business. But that's the nature of an evolving business; you must be willing to continually reinvent yourself to ensure that you stay in the game and do whatever it takes to succeed.

Providing Your Customers with an Exceptional Experience

What makes the difference between a good company and a great one? The answer, in large part, boils down to how well that company treats their customers. If you are in the people business—and *everyone* is, to some extent—then your highest priority should be to do whatever it takes to exceed your customers' expectations—today. It doesn't matter if your company is a hardware store, restaurant, online provider, or a health spa— you can create countless ways to provide your customers with an exceptional experience. Remember, no matter how big your organization is, its success is based on the sum total of interactions with every customer . . . every day.

> *A major key to success of any business in today's competitive environment is to never lose sight of the fact that your number one goal is to please your customers.*
>
> —Edgar A. Falk

Exceeding Expectations at Work

Exceeding expectations is a powerful way to influence others and gain your peers' and customers' respect. Here are seven practical ideas that are sure to help you stand out at your workplace:

1. Arrive early and stay late. Not once, but often enough to make it a habit.
2. Become the most optimistic person at your place of business. Optimism is a choice, and it should be your choice to radiate excitement and enthusiasm from the time you wake up until you go to bed at night.
3. Do each and every task as if the cameras are rolling and all eyes are on you. Take pride in what you do.
4. Once you make a decision—be it large or small—take some kind of specific action toward its realization.

5. Align yourself with a daily commitment to raising the bar of excellence for yourself and those around you.
6. Take great joy in the triumphs of others, and show compassion toward their disappointments.
7. Always be there to offer assistance and a hand up to your internal and external customers.

Step 2:
Commit to Daily
Measurable
Improvement

Without change there is no innovation, creativity, or incentive for improvement. Those who initiate change will have a better opportunity to manage the change that is inevitable.

—William Pollard

The World of Kaizen

While harnessing the power of measurable improvement might not be a cutting-edge idea, it certainly has teeth. For decades, the Japanese have practiced the concept of "kaizen," which simply means "improvement." W. Edwards Deming—a U.S. business-man who taught the Japanese about quality during the country's recovery after World War II—made the term of business legend. Kaizen is known in the corporate world as a strategy usually associated with activities that continually improve all functions of a business, from the CEO to manufacturing level employees, from assembly line workers to management. Kaizen's goal is to improve standardized activities and processes while eliminating business waste, a concept that makes the idea of *measurable improvement* more relevant than ever. After all, the holy grail of business in the twenty-first century is discovering ways to become more efficient.

Albert Einstein once said, "The most powerful force in the universe is compound interest." Patience and long-term focus are required in order for the power of compound interest to take effect; and so it is with kaizen. Whether you're an athlete, an entertainer, a corporate global leader, or a mom-and-pop start-up—practicing kaizen will help you deliver small improvements that will yield large results in the form of compound productivity and stellar results.

There is always room for improvement, you know—it's the biggest room in the house.

—Louise Heath Leber

The World's Funniest Virtuoso Guitarist

Mike Rayburn is the perfect example of how a commitment to continual improvement can elicit extraordinary success. I first met Mike in 1987 at an NACA (National Association for Campus Activities) convention in Birmingham, Alabama, where hundreds of college activities buyers had gathered to choose campus performers. It was Mike's first college showcase, and the entire audience—including myself—was amazed by not only his virtuosic guitar abilities, but also his uproarious humor.

During that first year, Mike charged just $275 a show. But he quickly became a favorite on the college scene, performing 100-plus campuses each year, and that kind of demand upped his fee rapidly. For the next 16 years, Mike Rayburn dominated the college entertainment scene.

Mike and I have been best of friends since that day we met in Birmingham, and we often act as sounding boards for each other as we've navigated our careers through the tumultuous entertainment industry. We've also debated endlessly on what it takes to be a successful performer. I would do my best to convince him that the only way to achieve national success is to have a hit record, or land a lucky appearance on TV. Mike, on the other hand, staunchly believes that consistently making incremental improvements—and honing his show day after day—results in a successful and prosperous career. And he was right!

In the same way that a bodybuilder works out daily, Mike practices every element of his show on a regular basis. He sees every second on stage as precious and invaluable—the same way that business owners should see every second of a customer's time. He is on a never-ending quest to cut the weaker moments from his show, and cram it with only the best material. Mike is concerned with even the smallest of details; he eliminates what he's deemed to be a few unnecessary words from a joke in order to get to the punch line faster. Mike's constant desire to give his audience the best has landed him at the top of his game; and business is good. In 20 years, Mike's fee for each show has gone up by more than 3,000 percent— which reflects nicely in his yearly income. These days, you can find him headlining on the Las Vegas Strip and performing at huge corporate events, where he is treated like a king and paid to fly in and perform for an hour.

Yes, Mike Rayburn is extremely talented, but so are many others who had their 15 minutes of fame, only to be forgotten within a few years. Mike's approach reminds me of the fable about the tortoise and the hare. While Mike's strategy is admittedly slow and steady, his sheer consistency in improving a little each day has put his career on a perpetual and powerful climb since the day I met him. Mike is different from other performers because he embraces show business as a *business*. His commitment to continual and measurable improvement—along with some well-honed talent—has made Mike Rayburn a huge financial success in what is undeniably a tough industry.

> *Champions do not become champions when they win the event, but in the hours, weeks, months and years they spend preparing for it. The victorious performance itself is merely the demonstration of their championship character.*
>
> —T. Alan Armstrong

90 Dark Horse Rules

Ten years ago, I created our first company manual for Dark Horse Recording, and every year since then I have revised it to specify our procedures with increasingly greater detail. By making incremental improvements on both a daily and yearly basis, we have evolved into a different business than when we started. Our commitment to constant forward motion, improving technologically, putting more efficient systems in place, and better serving our customers is the only reason we're still in business. Perhaps some of the following list of 90 concepts/rules will apply to your company.

1. Your core responsibility at Dark Horse is to help our guests have a memorable experience. Think of Dark Horse as a beautiful getaway, where it's your mission to make all guests feel at home.

2. Always answer the phone with warmth and enthusiasm. Make our clients feel at ease and let them know you're happy they called.

3. Slow down and speak distinctly when answering the phone.

4. If a call comes in for Tim (the Dark Horse manager) while he's not here, ask the client if it is a booking-related call and if we can get back to them shortly. Then do what*ever it takes* to track Tim down. If you can't find him, then call me—whether I'm in town or not. *Nothing* is more important than immediately responding to a caller interested in a potential booking.

5. Stop whatever you are doing when a client arrives and help them bring in their instruments and baggage. Offer to bring them where they need to go; don't just point.

6. Every time a guest walks through our doors, escort them into the kitchen/lounge, open the refrigerator, and offer them juices, water, or soft drinks. Then offer them coffee, hot tea, bagels, or snacks. They may be tired, hungry, or thirsty, so let this be an opportunity for them to experience refuge and rejuvenation upon arriving at Dark Horse.

7. Constantly arrange chairs and stools in kitchens, lounges, and media room into place.

8. Anytime you see a hand towel, pillow, bar of soap, or anything else that's out of place, it's your job to readjust.

9. When our guests request water, explain that we now serve reverse-osmosis water instead of bottled water because it is purer and doesn't waste plastic bottles.

10. Introduce yourself by giving your name; no jokes, no flirting, no cuteness.

11. Once you've offered food and drink, speak only when spoken to.

(continued)

(Continued)

12. Give guests their space when they are in the kitchens or lounges. Try to be invisible.
13. Try to avoid being in the same place as our guests (unless they've requested your presence for some reason), so that they will have a greater sense of privacy.
14. When in the studios, never inject your personal thoughts or taste about their music.
15. Handle every piece of equipment with care and respect. This will send a message that we care about everything at Dark Horse—especially their project.
16. Make sure that every glass, plate, and piece of silverware is carefully organized and properly displayed for our clients.
17. Continually arrange bagels, snacks, fruit, and all other food so it is pleasing to look at.
18. Constantly check all microwaves, refrigerators, stoves, and counters and make sure they are clean.
19. Learn the specific arrangements in which sweeteners, coffee grinder, toasters, and so forth are to be displayed, and then take pride in keeping them that way.
20. Check and empty all garbage cans every hour and recycle bins as needed.
21. Restock all refrigerators every hour. Make sure that all drinks are perfectly organized with labels facing forward.
22. Make certain that every bathroom has fresh "neatly rolled hand towels," fresh soap, and three spare rolls of toilet tissue. Check on this every hour.
23. When you ask a guest, "How's everything?" or "How is your session going?" *listen* to the answer and report any negative comments (no matter how seemingly insignificant) to studio manager.
24. Report any guest complaints or negative comments—no matter how seemingly insignificant—to studio manager.
25. Never say "I don't know" to any question without following it with, "I'll find out."

26. Know the details of the session before guests arrive. Do not ask, "What's going on today?" in front of clients.
27. If you see cobwebs, insects, or dirt that's been tracked in, clean it up on the spot.
28. Straighten/dust pictures and record plaques on every floor in every building on a daily basis.
29. Learn the specific ways that the studios and lounges are to be arranged, and then take pride in keeping them that way. Attention to detail is everything.
30. Pencils, pens, and sharpies are to be displayed at all 17 phone stations in a specific way: ten sharpened pencils in cup #1, five matching ballpoint pens in cup #2, and a red, black, and blue sharpie along with two yellow highlighters in cup #3.
31. When you are walking across the grounds, driveways, and parking areas, take ownership and pick up small pieces of trash, cigarette butts, and so forth.
32. Know how to use fax machines, copy machines, and be knowledgeable about all supplies that are stocked so that you are ready to help when a guest needs assistance with these things.
33. Never use the same mug for a second drink when a guest requests more coffee.
34. We are a triple bottom line company; we care about the environment and our local community as well as making a profit. Therefore, we recycle everything. If you spot plastic bottles and aluminum cans in trash bins, please pull them out and place them in the correct recycling bins.
35. Never make a client feel bad for not recycling. Quietly lead by example.
36. Do not have a personal conversation with another staff or intern within earshot of our guests.
37. Do not eat or drink in plain view of Dark Horse guests.
38. If you are a smoker, make sure you don't reek from cigarettes. Nonsmokers don't want to smell it.

(continued)

(Continued)

39. Do not drink alcohol on the job, even if invited by the guests. "Not when I'm on duty" will suffice.
40. Address men as "Sir," and women as "Ma'am."
41. Saying "No problem" is a problem. It has a tone of insincerity or sarcasm. "My pleasure" or "You're welcome" will do.
42. Do not compliment a guest's attire, hairstyle, or makeup, as doing so might insult someone else.
43. Your performance, passion, and level of enthusiasm should remain consistent no matter what project you are involved in and regardless if you are being paid.
44. Do not discuss your own listening preferences; it might insult or degrade a customer's.
45. *Do not curse*, no matter how young or hip the guests, and even if our guests are doing it.
46. Never acknowledge any one guest over and above any other. All guests are equal.
47. Do not gossip about co-workers or guests *ever*.
48. When answering phones, make every effort to pick up at a station where you will not interrupt or intrude on a guest's space.
49. Never keep any caller on hold for more than 20 seconds without returning to them and asking if they would mind continuing to hold.
50. Make sure that phone station ringers are turned off in studios when clients are recording.
51. Develop a detailed understanding of the gear-patching requirements in each studio. When a guest asks you to bring up a CD or patch in a compressor or preamp, you'll give them the impression that you know what you're doing.
52. Lend a hand anytime you see an opportunity to help a guest, staff member, or intern.
53. Do not ignore a guest because you are assigned to a different project. Get involved.
54. Do not ignore obvious chores because you are assigned to a different project. Get involved.

55. Do not judge any request—whether it is for food, or any eccentric demand of any kind.
56. No matter what a guest requests, say yes with enthusiasm and then proceed to fulfill it if it is doable.
57. Always make eye contact.
58. Never gossip about or blame other staff, interns, or the studio when things aren't going right.
59. Never allow a guest to pick up on negative vibes, even if the world is crumbling around you. Focus on solutions during times when things aren't going well.
60. Never talk about the price of studios to clients under any circumstances. Those duties are *solely* Tim's responsibility.
61. *Never* discuss what bookings you *think* are on the studio calendar, because these things change daily. Tim is the *only* keeper of the calendar.
62. If someone calls asking about what bookings are on the calendar, say "Sorry I don't know; let me put you in touch with Tim."
63. When taking phone calls, carefully print each message on the phone answering pads, then see they are delivered to the correct person, or put into the appropriate box. Use pen, not pencil.
64. Do not answer the phone unless you know how all the various transfers are accomplished.
65. If a client offers to settle payment with you, answer, "Tim is the only one who can take care of that"; then track him down.
66. If you're vacuuming when clients walk in, stop until a later, more convenient time when it won't be intrusive to our guests. Shhhhhhhh!
67. When crises arise, respond with a sense of extreme urgency.
68. If someone asks to hear your life story, keep it short.
69. When someone requests water, ask if they would like it in a glass, over ice, or in a sports bottle.
70. Make it your business to know what microphones are available for the session you are involved in.

(continued)

(Continued)

71. Never disappear.
72. Interns do not delegate to other interns unless you are the "in-charge" intern. If you are the in-charge intern, all delegations are your responsibility.
73. When using tools, office supplies, or anything else, put them back the way you found them.
74. If you drip or spill something, clean it up or replace it immediately.
75. Use client's break-times as an opportunity to straighten and clean.
76. When a guest asks you to go pick up food or run an errand that requires money, ask "How shall I pay for that?" Call Tim for instructions if they want us to pay and then put it on their invoice.
77. Be at the studio before our clients (even second engineers) arrive, and stay until after they leave at night—no matter how late they might work.
78. Keep your eye on all thermostats, especially in the studio to which you've been assigned. While our clients' comfort is paramount, if rooms or studios are not being used, turn off air-conditioning to be environmentally prudent.
79. Never patronize a guest who has a complaint or suggestion; listen, take it seriously, address it.
80. You may dress casually, but you must be neat and clean. No caps or T-shirts that draw attention.
81. Never hover around our guests or make them feel they are being watched. Remember, guests come to Dark Horse for peace, quiet, and privacy.
82. Do not show frustration. Your only mission is to serve the needs of our guests.
83. Help keep studios clean by putting all empty cases and case lids on the front deck.
84. Don't *ever* leave road cases with gear in them on the porches overnight. Bring them in before locking up, even if they clutter the hallways.

85. Even if you are assigned as second engineer, you are still responsible for cleaning the studio through the day.
86. Dark Horse Recording must always be showcase ready—*always*. Do not rest until buildings are 100 percent clean and organized.
87. Don't say you don't know what's going on. Make it your job to know what's on the Dark Horse calendar for the day. When someone calls, you'll know who's recording where.
88. Even if you have no idea how to solve a problem, quickly find someone who can.
89. Do not interrupt a conversation for any reason.
90. Demonstrate your passion for being involved in the music industry. That passion will be contagious to our clients, especially nonprofessionals.

Repetition of the same thought or physical action develops into a habit which, repeated frequently enough, becomes an automatic reflex.

—Dr. Norman Vincent Peale

Like any hospitality business, our ability to provide our guests with memorable experiences requires attention to detail coupled with a steadfast commitment to improve. This becomes the fuel that drives growth. Again—no matter what your company or role, consistently striving to improve will give you the competitive edge. Put simply: There's no better strategy for achieving long-term sustainability than aspiring to be better today than you were yesterday.

To achieve extraordinary results you must be disciplined and consistent and willing to make small efforts of improvement.

Step 3:
Develop an
Accountability
Matrix

We are made wise not by the recollection of our past, but by the responsibility for our future.

—George Bernard Shaw

Mission Critical

Figuring out and documenting who in your organization is accountable for key business processes certainly isn't the sexiest job in the world. However, creating an accountability matrix is essential to problem-avoidance and achieving repeatable success. It's a tool that requires you to identify and document every process and function that's essential to your business's operations. Often called "mission critical" functions, these procedures are absolutely vital to your business's productivity. Like any living organism, a company's number one goal is to sustain its own existence. However, many businesses manage to sustain themselves year after year, and never really go anywhere or make any money. So the second goal after sustainability is *profitability*. And somebody—a real live human being—must be responsible for the day-to-day functions and intermediate tasks that make sustainability and profitability possible.

Creating an accountability matrix is a simple three-step process:

1. You must examine every process, function, and task and determine what's critical for sustainability and essential for profitability.
2. You have to figure out who in your organization is responsible for each of these areas.
3. You must *inform* these individuals that they are responsible.

Bernie's $65-Billion Scam

In 2009, David Kotz—head of the Securities and Exchange Commission's (SEC) Office of Inspector General—issued a 477-page report that tried to explain how his organization missed catching notorious wealth management operator-turned criminal Bernie Madoff's Ponzi scheme. The report could have been a one-pager. Based on news reports of the scandal, one might assume that Madoff simply turned himself in one day, and that the SEC was as shocked to hear about his underhanded, illegal tactics as Madoff's investors were. But that was not the case.

For 17 years, various SEC offices had been receiving tips that something was up with Madoff's company, and investigated him time and again. Although the Boston branch got many of the best tips, since Madoff's operations were in New York, they weren't the office accountable for follow-through. The SEC's New England Regional Office conducted several investigations, yet each time they looked into specific, technical issues, not a single one of them was "responsible" for discovering if Bernie was indeed running a Ponzi scheme. And, as we all know now, they didn't, causing thousands of people to lose billions due to the SEC's negligence.

The entire 477-page report outlines in excruciating detail how each investigation was handled. The bottom line—and the reason that the entire report could be condensed to one page—is that there was never a *single individual* in the SEC responsible for keeping an eye out for Ponzi schemes. If there had been, maybe Bernie would have been caught long before he gave himself up. For this reason, nobody at the SEC has been fired for not catching Madoff. You can't fire people if you can't identify who's responsible, and nobody at the SEC was responsible. Nobody.

> *The price of greatness is responsibility.*
>   —Winston Churchill

The Buck Stops Here

President Harry Truman took a much different approach than the SEC during his tenure as U.S. President. Truman is famous for placing a sign on his desk in the Oval Office that said, "The Buck Stops Here." He recognized that ultimately *he* was in charge of the federal government and responsible for everything that went right—or wrong. Truman, for example, made the tough decision to drop two atomic bombs on Japan and end the war. I can't begin to think of a more difficult decision than that.

And whether you have a sign on your desk or not—the same
is true for you. When most enterprises fail, the higher ups frequently claim they were not in the know or responsible because
they weren't "in the loop." In other words, they keep passing
the buck. That's why developing an accountability matrix into
your organization simply makes good business sense.

Whose Responsibility Is It?

Whether you own a business or manage someone else's company, whatever happens is eventually *your* responsibility. I often
emphasize this point in my keynote speeches by getting the audience to participate. I'll say "I can tell you unequivocally that
leading my business Dark Horse Recording to success comes
down to taking responsibility. So let me ask you . . . if my staff
or interns don't answer the phone in a warm and enthusiastic
voice, who's responsibility is it?" And the audience will yell "It's
yours!" Then I'll run through a handfull of scenarios/crises that
any business owner has faced, finishing up with, "If my bills
don't get paid . . . If my invoices don't get collected . . . If light-
ning strikes and wipes out my computer memory, not in my
office, but down in Stephanie's (our bookkeeper) office and her
files weren't backed up . . . whose responsibility is it?" And once
again everyone yells "It's yours!" Setting up an accountability
matrix for your company is easy. Simply use a spreadsheet and
make a list of each mission critical function or process. Next,
assign each one to a *specific person*. Finally, and most importantly,
let them know *they* are the one person responsible for that process. You can make it more complicated if you want, but most
are just this simple.

Cooking the Books

The fall of Enron is one of the most disturbing examples of a company "dressing up" (or lying about) their bottom line to show healthy profits, when they were in fact *losing* money. Accounting firm Arthur Andersen handled Enron's finances, and was once the world's largest accounting firm—until it imploded during the Enron scandal. In 2002, the firm voluntarily surrendered its licenses to practice as Certified Public Accountants after being found guilty of turning a blind eye as Ken Lay and a few others were busy cooking the books. Their refusal to be held accountable (no pun intended) and outright greed resulted in the loss of 85,000 jobs, plus millions in pensions and retirements.

Healthy responsibility is defined as taking 100 percent responsibility for yourself while inspiring others to take 100 percent responsibility.
—Gay Hendricks

Dodging Bullets

We are living in a time where top executives and even CEOs continually dodge the bullets of responsibility. Our financial crisis and near global collapse came about in large part because companies like Lehman Brothers, Enron, WorldCom, and AIG seem to have no accountability matrix in place. When there was so much fast money to be made, accountants, money managers, and investors simply looked the other way. For instance, once again the SEC missed numerous red flags on Allen Stanford of the Stanford Financial Group, much as they did with Bernie

Madoff. According to the *New York Times*, the SEC found several securities violations over the years, but each time the regulators ultimately let the company off with relatively small fines. There was no one person who was responsible, and the behavior of big companies who aren't willing to be accountable is an issue that has people outraged.

FEMA's Lack of Accountability

Hurricane Katrina hit New Orleans in August of 2005, and caused more than 50 breaches in drainage canal levees—resulting in the worst engineering disaster in the history of the United States. Two days later, 80 percent of New Orleans was flooded, with some parts under 15 feet of water. Federal Emergency Management Agency's (FEMA) director Michael Brown was the only executive to get fired because of his organization's lack of response to this disaster, but other members of this group failed to take responsibility as well. It's now painfully obvious that FEMA had no matrix of accountability in place, didn't take rapid or concrete enough action—and as a result, countless people were left helpless and homeless. The complete and utter failure to successfully respond to the magnitude of the New Orleans crisis after Hurricane Katrina in large part came down to FEMA's lack of accountability, which was universally acknowledged to have been abysmal.

Because of the debacle that followed Hurricane Katrina, the Disaster Accountability Project was founded to improve FEMA, American Red Cross, and the other government agencies and nonprofit organizations responsible for disaster preparedness, response, relief, and recovery. In other words, the Disaster Accountability Project was founded to, well, to help bring a higher level of *accountability* to help ensure that a repeat of FEMA's failure to respond to the next disaster never happens again.

> *He who refuses to embrace a unique opportunity loses the prize as surely as if he had tried and failed.*
>
> —William James

Become Extraordinary

Your success in business and life will always be in direct proportion to the level of responsibility you take for your choices and decisions. Although many people want to wear the cloak of leadership, with it comes the burden of responsibility. Remember, failure to hit the bull's-eye is never the target; that's why successful leaders focus on responsibility over blame. Deepening your commitment by creating a personal accountability/ responsibility matrix means that you've made a decision to become extraordinary.

Who *Does* Take Responsibility?

While this book was being readied for press, one of my editors asked if I couldn't, at this point in the book, cite at least a few examples of companies where the leaders *do* take responsibility. That's easy: just look at any successful business—from the

Fortune 500 on down to the corner store. If the business is successful, you better believe there is somebody inside taking responsibility. The failures we hear the most about are at companies and organizations where responsibility is avoided. Companies with responsible leaders don't always avoid problems, but they do tend to survive them . . . so can you.

Step 4:
Reinvigorate
Your Organization
Through
Multidimensional
Thinking

If you want to make an apple pie from scratch, you must first create the universe.

—Carl Sagan

Functioning on Multiple Levels

The movie *Contact* tells the story of an astronomer (played by Jodi Foster) who has devoted her life to making contact with life beyond Earth. When she discovers a transmission signal from 28 light years away, the entire world is spellbound by the data she receives. Teams of scientists attempt to decipher the messages, but can't understand how the two-dimensional pages line up.

Eventually, Foster's mentor deduces that "an alien intelligence has got to be more advanced. That means efficiency, functioning on multiple levels and in *multiple dimensions.*" Lo and behold—he puts the pages from the alien civilization together in a three-dimensional form, and begins to understand the messages they're receiving.

Yes, it's a science fiction movie, but there's a good point to be made. As we move forward and develop more efficient ways of doing business, we must discover how to function on multiple levels and think in multidimensional terms. Whether it's finding ways to reuse waste, reducing energy costs, or simply not making left-hand turns, there are countless methods for conducting business creatively.

> *The creative is the place where no one else has ever been. You have to leave the city of your comfort and go into the wilderness of your intuition. What you'll discover will be wonderful. What you'll discover is yourself.*
>
> —Alan Alda

Low-Tech Multidimensional Thinking

One of the best examples of thinking outside the box actually involves a *real* box.

In the early twentieth century, Henry Ford's Model T ushered in a new era for our country by putting America on wheels. The engines of these cars used carburetors that Ford purchased from another company; and he was particular about the box the carburetor was shipped in. It had to be made from a particular kind of wood with each board a specific size, and Ford also specified where each nail hole had to be. The carburetor company probably thought Henry Ford was just being eccentric, but complied since he was their biggest customer. They supplied not only the carburetor, but shipped it as well in a wooden box built to Ford's precise specifications. What they didn't know was that Ford had his workers disassemble the boxes in which the carburetors were shipped and use the wood as the floorboards of the Model T. This way, he didn't have to have a separate carpenter shop or buy wood for the floorboards. The parts were fragile and had to be shipped in a good box, and his workers would have to take the boxes apart to get the carburetor out. So why not use the box and the existing labor in an unconventional way to solve a need at no additional cost? That is *true* "multidimensional" thinking.

Henry Ford had introduced sustainability to business before there was even a word to describe it. To this day, he is still revered in business schools for this kind of multidimensional and original thinking. Consider how you might incorporate this kind of thinking into *your* company; what creative approaches can you use to reduce waste and save money for your business?

> *When I am working on a problem I never think about beauty. I only think about how to solve the problem. But when I have finished, if the solution is not beautiful, I know it is wrong.*
> —Buckminster Fuller

Thinking Outside the Box

Multidimensional thinking might also be referred to as "*thinking outside the box.*" There's a story about a Disney management consultant who drew a box made up of nine dots:

Imagination is more important than knowledge.

—Albert Einstein

The challenge was to link all the dots using no more than four straight lines and without lifting the pen. Try as you might, you can't do it if you confine your thinking to the "box"—since there really is *no box*. Your brain creates the box around the drawing, and restricts your ability to solve the problem. The solution, of course, is to think outside the box.

On the next page you might be surprised at the simplicity of the solution to this puzzle.

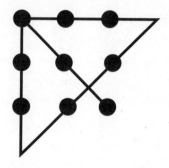

Management consultants still use this example when trying to get companies to look at problems in a new, unconventional way. Taco Bell has enjoyed a successful marketing campaign using the play on words "think outside the bun."

The average business executive has spent between 1,000 and 10,000 hours formally learning economics, history, languages, literature, mathematics, and political science! The same executive has spent less than ten hours learning about creative thinking!

—Tony Buzan

The Fourth Dimension

Let's take this multidimensional concept one-step further and consider the all-important dimension of *time*. All financial calculations include time; it changes the cost and value of everything. Interest, for example, is rent on money over time. The faster you pay back the loan, the less it will cost. In fact, the faster you do *anything*, the less it usually costs.

Shipping company FedEx is a great example of an organization that recognizes how we now live in a culture based on speed. A profitable business is often about getting work done quickly and efficiently, thereby bringing your cost down and your revenues up. FedEx sees this, and has made billions of dollars helping people send packages faster.

> *The best way to have a good idea is to have lots of ideas.*
> —Linus Pauling

Faster Is Better—The American Way

The rest of the business world sees adopting "American methods" as utilizing a system of mass production where things get done quickly. McDonald's didn't get to be the world's largest restaurant chain making the "best" hamburger; they got there by making the fastest hamburger. The business is, after all, *fast food*. Americans drink instant coffee, eat instant oatmeal, and use the microwave for *everything*, not because these taste "better" but because they are faster; and in most markets, faster is better. We want to be faster to market; faster to get out of a line of business when it's no longer profitable; faster than your competitor in response to changes—faster, period.

> *The only sustainable competitive advantage comes from out-innovating the competition!*
> —Tom Peters

A Beautiful Tool

In 1947, German chemist Dr. Hans Goldschmidt invented a woodworking tool that was decades ahead of its time. It was a combination table saw, lathe, disc sander, drill press, and band saw; a beautiful example of multidivisional thinking. Growing up, I remember two of my neighbors who displayed this Shopsmith as the centerpiece in their home workshop. And for good reason—the simple machine Goldschmidt designed can perform multiple functions with ease, allowing a carpenter to build virtually anything, yet it can be stored in the space of a bicycle.

Sixty years later, Dr. Goldschmidt's invention is as relevant as ever; and the company he founded still sells this tool to woodworking enthusiasts all over the world. More than 600,000 Shopsmiths have been sold worldwide and most are still in use today, serving their owners just as they did when they were new. The company's marketing promise "the tool you start with—the system you grow with." In the last 60 years there have been thousands of woodworking tools brought to market, but none has stood the test of time the way the Shopsmith has. And in that time the Shopsmith's timeless design hasn't changed a bit.

Creativity requires the courage to let go of certainties.
—Erich Fromm

Stretching the Limits of What Is Possible

As we continue our journey into the twenty-first century, we must stretch the limits of possibility, and develop efficient products that function on multiple levels. Twenty-five years ago, who could have imagined that computers would have seemingly infinite applications, such as architecture, photography, and music. Entrepreneurs as diverse as Henry Ford and Steve Jobs have produced multidimensional products, which not only produced vast fortunes, but changed the landscape of how we live for the better. Multidimensional thinking starts by asking "what if and why not" and breaking down self imposed limitations to create business models that function on multiple levels simultaneously.

There is nothing in a caterpillar that tells you it's going to be a butterfly.

—Buckminster Fuller

Step 5:
Create a
Culture of
Shared Sacrifice

Self-sacrifice is the real miracle out of which all the reported miracles grow.

—Ralph Waldo Emerson

A New Form of Patriotism

Certain facts are self-evident. The more you learn about population growth versus resource depletion, the more you'll want to continually find ways to make your business more efficient in order to succeed. There are many once-thriving companies that are now on life support—all because they didn't evolve with the times. In some cases, those companies' leaders simply weren't willing to step out of their comfort zone and look beyond the next quarterly shareholders meeting. Take the big three automakers, for example. When Ford, GM, and Chrysler had to plead with Congress for $25 billion in bailout money to avoid bankruptcy, their executives arrived in Washington aboard private jets.

I might not be qualified to be CEO of an automobile company, but I can't imagine being so out of touch, arrogant, and just plain stupid to do that. *Even* if they weren't sincere, flying coach on Southwest Airlines to get there would have been worth its weight in gold in political capital.

> *The gem cannot be polished without friction, nor man perfected without trials.*
>
> —Chinese Proverb

"Close that Refrigerator! You're Running Up the Electric Bill"

My grandparents lived through the Great Depression, and like most people of that generation, they experienced the collective pain and suffering that everyone else endured. During the worst of it, unemployment rose to almost 25 percent; there were few agencies and programs in place to help the hungry, the sick, and the homeless. All that personal devastation shaped Emil and Ruby Crow's character with a powerful work ethic, a sense of frugality, and a spirit of gratefulness. Put simply, they learned how to make do with less.

My grandfather Emil Crow did quite well for himself, and eventually worked his way up to becoming a distributor for a small Texas company called Amalie Motor Oil. In fact, he did well enough to purchase a vacation getaway, a lake house that he and my grandmother would visit on the weekends. But the scars from the Great Depression ran deep and permeated their lifestyle in every way. The Crows didn't believe in debt of any kind (other than house payments), so they saved every penny, and lived way below their means.

I remember visiting them as a teenager and going into the kitchen to grab something to eat. I would open the refrigerator door and after about two seconds my grandmother would sound out, "Close that door, you're running up the electric bill!" That concern for every penny was reflected in their financial stability, which is so rare to see in this century. When was the last time you observed someone concerned about how long the refrigerator door stayed open? I rest my case.

> *Happiness can be defined, in part at least, as the fruit of desire and ability to sacrifice what we want now for what we want eventually.*
> —Stephen R. Covey

More than a Feeling

Shared sacrifice is more than a business idea or strategy; it's a mindset and way of living. It's something that my grandparents— and all Americans who suffered the Great Depression—certainly understood. However, our culture nowadays is concerned with "having it all" no matter what the cost. Instead of cutting back to pull ourselves out of debt, we continue to overextend.

What does this have to do with business? *Everything!* What's reflected in our personal lives is also reflected in the way we run our companies. Companies like AIG, Lehman Brothers, Bear Sterns, Merrill Lynch, and Countrywide Mortgage all needed to be bought out or bailed out because of how they mishandled these institutions. "Mishandling" is actually a gross understatement in many cases as to what actually occurred. The indisputable reality is that many top executives' personal greed led to so much bloat and corruption that it was merely a matter of time before the house of cards would fall. They got caught up in the idea that there was easy money to be made, but as we all now know, the bubble burst and created a financial Pearl Harbor that has left millions of Americans out of work and caused countless small businesses to suffer or close.

I prayed for twenty years but received no answer until I prayed with my legs.

—Frederick Douglass

The Power of Sacrifice

A month after the actual bombing of Pearl Harbor in December 1941, President Roosevelt delivered a speech to the American people where he promised to have 100,000 combat airplanes and 75,000 tanks built in the following year. That sounded like an outrageous fantasy to everyone, especially to the Nazis. They thought it was just so much propaganda and believed Americans to be soft and unwilling to sacrifice and put "guns before butter" (a common phrase used back then).

Roosevelt's speech personified leadership at its best. He was tough, inspiring, and gave people a sense of united purpose in his dramatic call to pull together and sacrifice for the common good. People were asked to conserve everything, and the United States began rationing tires, automobiles, gasoline, sugar, coffee, stoves, shoes, meat, lard, shortening and oils, and, of course, butter to supply the war effort. They planted "Victory Gardens" to conserve food, an idea that was so successful that there was an estimated 20 million families with Victory Gardens—which produced 40 percent of America's vegetables—by 1945.

Back then, people were willing to sacrifice a bit of the bottom line, precious time, and work hard, because they had a common enemy and mission: to keep our country's freedom at all cost. That undertaking brought our economy through the war, and immediately into an era of relative prosperity and growth. And it all began with simple, heartfelt gestures and actions, like people collecting old aluminum pots, steel cans, and scrap copper to provide more ammunition for the soldiers. Rationing meant sacrifices for worker bees and CEOs alike, and ration stamps became a kind of currency with each family. Few people complained, because they knew it was the men and women in uniform who were making the greater sacrifice.

The important thing is this: to be able at any moment to sacrifice what we are for what we could become.

—Charles Dubois

The Unstoppable American Spirit

The United States became the Arsenal of Democracy as we built even more tanks and planes than Roosevelt had promised. There was a spirit of national purpose as Britain was literally transformed to a storage depot for vast quantities of U.S.-made weaponry. When the heat was on, U.S. citizens responded with a "whatever it takes" commitment of shared sacrifice. That proved we had what it takes to break through and surpass what conventional wisdom (and our enemies) imagined was possible.

It took an extraordinary—and tragic—event like Pearl Harbor to show what we were really made of, and a total commitment from the President down to the shift worker on the defense plant factory floor. We "were in it to win it." There was simply no strategy the enemy could employ that could keep the United States from winning. Shared sacrifice was at the core of U.S. success in World War II, which proved we are inherently capable of becoming an unstoppable force when the U.S. spirit is truly put to the test.

As we contemplate how to be more competitive—to stretch our resources and create sustainable business models—we can learn some valuable business lessons from the inspiring examples of sacrifice from World War II. Encourage your colleagues to paint far outside the lines to discover more efficient methods of making business better today than it was yesterday. Lead with a sense of urgency. Time, not money, is your most precious resource. Be bold. Encourage everyone in your organization to share in the sacrifices, but make sure that you are at the front of the line leading the troops.

A Tale of Two Leaders

Donald Carty and Lee Iacocca have each held positions that entailed staggering levels of responsibility. When Carty was CEO of American Airlines and Iacocca head of Chrysler, both faced the threat of bankruptcy and had to respond to an economic crisis. However, that's where the parallels end. Their ability to navigate the treacherous waters of revitalizing their companies and inspire employees to do more for less became one's undoing—and the other's unprecedented triumph.

At first, it was called Carty's "historic" victory—the biggest consensual airline restructuring ever. In the wake of the 9/11 attacks, American Airlines was facing hard times. In an effort to keep the airline out of bankruptcy in 2003, Carty made a plea for shared sacrifice to the labor unions, and by a narrow vote the unions accepted $1.62 billion worth of pay concessions.

Then came Carty's megablunder when, just a few days later, the deal unraveled as unions learned that airline executives were keeping $41 million in retention bonuses. As you can imagine, there was total outrage from the workers who were in the trenches and who actually kept the mammoth airline running. Several board members were outraged as well and called for Carty's resignation. On April 24, 2003, he stepped down. Donald Carty paid a bigger price for his arrogance and hypocritical leadership than he ever possibly imagined.

How can you expect your most important and invaluable resource—your employees—to arrive early, stay late, give up salary and perks, then put in 110 percent, if they don't see you doing the same? Remember: a leader leads by example *whether he intends to or not.*

On the other end of the spectrum is Lee Iacocca, who credits saving Chrysler for one reason: everyone shared in the sacrifice, starting with him. After reducing his salary to $1 a year, he requested that other Chrysler executives take similar cuts. *Then*, he approached the UAW (United Auto Workers) and asked the union to do the same. Over the period of a year and a half, the workers made an incredible $2.5 billion in concessions. As a result, Iacocca ultimately saved 170,000 jobs, upward of 600,000 once you factor in the ripple effect that bankruptcy would have had on distributors, suppliers, and so forth. In Iacocca's own words, "It was the workers' willingness to sacrifice that saved the company more than anything else." When Iacocca retired in 1992, Chrysler was the most profitable car company in the world, selling two and a half million cars and trucks each year—an achievement that would not have been possible without great leadership and the creation of a shared sacrifice culture.

It pays to think ahead. It wasn't raining when Noah built the ark.
—Howard Ruff

Sacrificing at Dark Horse Recording

These and other stories of sacrifice have inspired me to do the same at Dark Horse Recording in large and small ways. For starters I ask employees to watch all the thermostats like a hawk. We have 13 heating and air systems and simply turning the heat several degrees down in the winter and up in the summer saves approximately $6,000 a year. We use almost no disposable paper products, and we turn out the lights whenever possible. Several years ago, on any given day we would have sent a different intern or staffer to run each errand as the need arose. Now, in an effort to be more efficient, we plan further ahead. We write out everything we need on a sheet, including directions to *all* of the day's errands such as the post office, FedEx, hardware store, grocery store, and so forth. And although these may seem like insignificant examples, the rewards add up. My staff and I have deepened our commitment to sacrifice in order to save money, lower our carbon footprint, and thereby gaining a competitive edge.

If you're a business owner, you know there's always an endless list of projects to see through. That certainly holds true for me; so to make sure I don't lose ground during unsettling times, I put in longer hours. Most days I'm up at 4:30 AM to get a jump on the day—working on my latest book, or overseeing my three companies. My other team members have followed suit by consistently putting in additional hours as well. I can't remember the last time I heard anyone complain; the feeling is that we're all in this together.

In order for business to thrive during this perfect storm of a crumbling economy, energy crunch, and the falling housing market, you have to dig down deep to find the extra energy that's needed to gain the competitive edge. When it comes to business, personal leadership and commitment is up to each of us. Remember, what's good for our businesses will ultimately be good for our country and for the planet. As we face unprecedented challenges, we need leaders who are going to call for shared sacrifice once again, just like Roosevelt did in 1941.

At Dark Horse, each year we keep finding new ways to become more and more creative in order to maintain financial momentum. We have no choice but to get lean and mean in order to survive. We must continually find ways to do business more efficiently. This doesn't necessarily mean laying off employees, it may simply require you to decipher better ways to utilize each individual's personal strengths. Be the first to step up to the plate and make tangible sacrifices; when you do, others around you will join in the cause.

Concern should drive us into action, not into depression.
—Karen Horney

Where the Rubber Meets the Road

From the 30,000-foot view, it is easy to see that our global population growth is colliding with our constant need to conserve.
All of the ideas listed below will not only help you and your
company become more efficient, but each suggestion will save
you money. You'd be amazed at what is possible with a little
creativity. For example, we all can:

- Drive fuel-efficient cars.
- Carpool to work, and encourage your employees to do so.
- Drive a bit slower so your gas mileage will go up, and
  drive less.
- Recycle.
- Use less water.
- Use less plastic.
- Use less heat in the winter, and less air-conditioning in
  the summer.
- Unplug electronics that are on standby, which still use
  40 percent of the electricity as if they were on.
- Insulate your home and office.
- Use only compact fluorescent light bulbs and remember
  to turn off the lights.
- Use recycled products at home and at work.

Bottled Water—Quite the Scam

Are you aware that almost all brands of bottled water contain
nothing more than glorified tap water? And there is no gov-
ernmental agency in place to regulate this $11 billion industry.

Nonetheless, up until two years ago, my company Dark Horse Recording purchased approximately 800 bottles of water per month to keep our clients hydrated; that's almost 10,000 bottles per year! Then we installed a reverse-osmosis water system in each of our buildings, a one-time expense that cost about $2,000 for both systems. The first year alone we saved approximately $3,500, minus the initial purchase expense. It was a win-win. We saved money, started drinking healthier water, and canceled out the production of 10,000 plastic bottles per year. If my small mom-and-pop operation can achieve that much waste reduction, just imagine what much larger companies are capable of.

Be the Example

Whether you are talking about companies that employ tens of thousands like American Airlines and Chrysler, or a small "mom and pop" business like Dark Horse Recording, the same message applies: those in management positions must set the tone and *be the example* for shared sacrifice. That's the kind of leadership people are thirsty for. Once everyone in your organization sees you going without for the good of the company, then they will not only get on board, they will follow you to the ends of the earth.

Step 6: Transform Your Business Philosophy to a **Triple Bottom Line**

There's no business to be done on a dead planet.

—David Bower

The Importance of Triple Bottom Line

A triple bottom line (TBL) is an ongoing process that will help your company stay focused on running a more sustainable business, while demonstrating to your employees and local community that you're not only working toward riches, but toward the greater common good as well. Instead of focusing solely on the financial bottom line, there are two additional bottom lines to be considered here: the *social* and *environmental* ones. Triple bottom line is a business model of sustainability that balances economic success, social engagement, and environmental sustainability.

151

Although this phrase is new to many, it was actually first coined more than a decade ago in expert John Elkington's book *Cannibals with Forks*. John envisioned a business model where organizations focused on how they could affect their people and community and practice responsible stewardship over the environment, instead of concentrating solely on profit. A triple bottom line philosophy recognizes the need for healthy content people to staff a business, and thriving surroundings to sustain those people. In other words, if your business focuses on creating products as locally as possible and with fair labor while engaging in sustainable practices—then it will have a far better chance to stand the test of time.

We only have one planet in which to do business, so we best care for it.

Three Pillars that Comprise the Triple Bottom Line

A great leader's courage to fulfill his vision comes from passion, not position.

—John Maxwell

People

Companies that appreciate the value of their people acknowledge that they are indeed the lifeblood of an organization. Great organizations know this and make commitments to their employees that go far beyond a fair day's work for a fair day's pay. Some of these commitments include supporting the local community through donations, sponsorships, or various other projects focused on shared support. Companies that incorporate social responsibility into their business model not only help improve society, they also benefit themselves by enhancing relationships with customers, employees, and shareholders.

The most powerful weapon on earth is the human soul on fire.
—Field Marshall Ferdinand Foch

Planet

The second element to the triple bottom line equation is the planet. Every day brings more examples of businesses that enjoy double-digit growth while engaging in sustainable practices. It therefore only makes sense for large and small companies to commit to becoming efficient in every area going forward. Doing so will drive costs out of your business, while bringing revenues in. Carbon is the leading contributor to global warming. A company or individual's "carbon footprint" is a measure of how much greenhouse gases they are helping create, but carbon is mostly released by our use of energy and energy is (increasingly) expensive. Since energy is a cost, measuring your company's carbon footprint is simply a way of measuring costs. Many forward-thinking companies are calculating their carbon footprint at every stage; from shipping and administration, to sourcing raw materials, to production processes, and so on.

Choose your passion, not your pension.
—Denis Waitley,

Profit

Making a profit *at all costs* is never an effective strategy long term, yet greed has become synonymous with many corporations over the past several years. We live in an era where it's almost commonplace for CEOs to be serving time in jail for adopting illegal and greed-driven practices. Although these examples are somewhat extreme, they do paint a vivid example of what *not* to do. The theory behind the triple bottom line philosophy is that by paying attention to people, planet, and profits in harmony, you will not only increase profits, you will do so honestly.

At Dark Horse Recording we had coffee mugs created to send out to some our clients as thank you gifts with the following saying written on them: "Money is not the key to happiness . . . People with ten million dollars are no happier than people with nine." Although it's a phrase that makes most of us laugh—after all, $9 million should be more than enough to make anyone happy—that is apparently not the case. Many organizations are structured in such a way that each executive's job requires that they squeeze every last drop out of the department for which he or she is responsible. Taking that model of doing business to its logical conclusion, the company has no choice but to operate in a culture of greed. Instead, many CEOs and chairpeople need to think long and hard about how much "enough" is, then set out to create a sustainable and profitable bottom line that will stand the test of time.

> *Don't ask yourself what the world needs; ask yourself what makes you come alive.*
> *And then go and do that. Because what the world needs is people who have come alive.*
>
> —Harold Whitman

Ben & Jerry's

Ben & Jerry's is a shining example of this philosophy in action. Although they have become an icon for their "outside of the box" business practices and zany marketing campaigns, what really separates them from the pack is their commitment to people. The way that they treat their employees as well as the citizens who live in the communities where they do business has given them folk hero status as champions of social justice. With 500 stores and 8 factories worldwide, Ben & Jerry's could well be the poster child for the triple bottom line philosophy. Their mission statement is as follows:

We have a progressive, nonpartisan social mission that seeks to meet human needs and eliminate injustices in our local, national and international communities by integrating these concerns into our day-to-day business activities. Our focus is on children and families, the environment and sustainable agriculture on family farms.

Founded in 1978 in an old abandoned gas station in Burlington, Vermont, Ben Cohen, Jerry Greenfield, and friends furnished their original ice-cream establishment with a variety of rehabbed and refurbished items—a move that would serve as a forerunner to their long-standing, environmentally responsible practices. To celebrate their one-year anniversary, Ben and Jerry gave out free ice-cream cones all day long. This community event—and brilliant marketing practice—has become a worldwide, annual affair that continues to this day.

Every year since the company was founded has been accompanied by new practices and initiatives geared toward helping our planet and the people who inhabit it. You don't have to look any further than the frozen section in your grocery store to know that this beloved brand sells *a lot* of ice cream. Their 2008 sales exceeded $300 million, and in response they gave back millions of dollars in the forms of grants, scholarships, and community action support to individuals and organizations all over the world. Ben & Jerry's success speaks volumes to the notion of taking care of the people who take care of your company. Keep this organization in mind as you rethink the way you do business and begin to start incorporating triple bottom line strategies into your company.

> *Every great dream begins with a dreamer. Always remember, you have within you the strength, the patience, and the passion to reach for the stars to change the world.*
> —Harriet Tubman

Stonyfield Farms

I recently had the opportunity to hear Stonyfield Farms CEO Gary Hirshberg speak on how sustainable practices can lead to profitability. As the leader of the world's largest organic yogurt producer—a $320 million corporation—this soft-spoken gentleman proceeded to blow me away as he described how he built his company by incorporating sustainable principles and practices, and how they have seen a more than 24 percent profit increase annually for the last 18 years. He laid out the most compelling case I've heard of on how making money and saving the planet can be accomplished simultaneously.

Hirshberg's book entitled *Stirring It Up* (which I highly recommend) contains the following quote: "After three decades straddling the worlds of business and environmental activism, I have concluded that the quickest and most powerful way to effect large-scale change is to use our purchasing power as both carrot and stick to prod business to get to work saving the planet." He then goes on to describe specific strategies and examples that can help other companies establish these kinds of practices and accomplish similar objectives. Hirshberg claims that Stonyfield has discovered—every step of the way—that sustainable practices are simply more profitable. If you want to see an example of cutting-edge triple bottom line business success, look no further than Stonyfield Farms.

> *"You don't get to choose how you're going to die. Or when. You can only decide how you're going to live. Now."*
>
> —Joan Baez

Newman's Own Triple Bottom Line

Unless you've been sleeping under a rock, you're probably familiar with—if not a fan of—late actor Paul Newman. In addition to starring in 57 movies and receiving a variety of accolades and awards for his acting—including an Academy Award for Best Actor for *The Color of Money*—he was the founder of the highly successful food company Newman's Own. For several years, Paul and his friend, author A.E. Hotchner, gave bottles of their homemade salad dressing to friends as holiday gifts. They would mix up a batch in Newman's basement and hand out old wine bottles filled with the dressing while Christmas caroling in their Westport, Connecticut neighborhood. One thing led to another, and the bottled dressing soon became a popular item in local gourmet shops. Newman and Hotchner reasoned that they were on to something, and decided to market their dressing as a vehicle to make profits to give to charitable foundations. So they each contributed $40,000 and in 1982, Newman's Own,

Inc. gave birth to its first product: Olive Oil & Vinegar Salad Dressing.

Other attempts at celebrity food products from Kenny Rogers' chicken to Tanya Tucker's salsa had rarely been successful in the past; therefore, Newman and Hotchner were counseled not to "get their hopes up." But any naysayers were quickly silenced when the dressing generated nearly a half-million dollars profit in the first year—all of which was donated to charity. Since that time, the company's products have come to include pasta sauce, lemonade, popcorn, salsa, and wine. As Newman's Own continued to grow, Newman and Hotchner remained steadfast in their commitment to donate all profits to charitable organizations. At the end of each year, Newman and Hotchner would sit down together, personally reviewing grant applications and then deciding which organizations needed aid most. At the time of Newman's death in 2008, his "own" donations had exceeded $250 million.

Newman's Own sets a perfect example of triple bottom line thinking. Their tongue-in-cheek mission statement—thought up by Newman himself—reads "Shameless Exploitation in Pursuit of the Common Good"; and in many ways, sets the tone for his company's purpose: a brilliant avenue for philanthropy at the highest level. Suppose that you're shopping in a grocery aisle and trying to decide among 10 different brands of salsa—each that comes in a multitude of flavors. You'll be considering three things: (1) Value: Is it a reasonable price? (2) Quality: Is it organic, healthy, and tasty? (3) Brand loyalty: Is it a company with which you wish to be associated? If you knew that purchasing one of those products would benefit a worthy cause because that particular company gives 100 percent of its profits to charity, you would choose Newman's Own hands down. Your decision would be largely based on the company's triple bottom line philosophy. It simply makes good business sense to incorporate these practices into your organization.

Only when the solutions to our global challenges are integrated with profitable and commercial strategies, will the business world get on board.

Endangered Species Chocolate

There are many people who feel that chocolate makes the world go around, and I happen to be one of them. Indianapolis-based Endangered Species Chocolate (ESC) is the number one organic chocolate manufacturer in the natural food category in the world; no small feat for a company less than two decades old! In 2003 and 2004, respectively, the company boasted monster growth of 46 percent and 30 percent. New owners moved Endangered Species from Portland to Indiana earlier this decade and the company grew from a $3-million-a-year "mom and pop" employing 18 people to a $16-million-a-year corporation that employs 60. Not only does Endangered Species Chocolate know how to make money, they also ensure that sustainable farming practices are utilized in providing them with their cocoa beans, because ESC practices an "ethical" trade policy. Ethical—as opposed to "fair" trade—means that ESC does more than merely pay a decent market price for their cocoa. The company also actively works to improve the living conditions of the farmers and the communities from which they source their product.

ESC buys all of their cocoa from small, family-owned farms to help sustain farming as a viable way of life. They also install water and purification systems, donate school and medical supplies, and provide new technological advancements for farms—*not* the standard by which typical and competing chocolate companies often operate. ESC has continued to grow at double-digit speed in scope and profitability throughout the past decade—all while donating 10 percent of their net profits to supporting endangered species, habitats, and humanity.

> *I am looking for a lot of men who have an infinite capacity to not know what can't be done.*
>
> —Henry Ford

TOMS Shoes

Imagine that you were able to establish a business model that can create commerce while changing the world at the same time, or build a company whose mission is so inspiring that droves of people, other companies, and even celebrities come out of the woodwork to help further your cause. Now imagine that you've designed an organization so revolutionary that within three years of its launch, you become the subject of numerous television shows, the recipient of awards—and even get invited to the White House. Well, Blake Mycoskie created just such a company. In 2006, the small-business entrepreneur from Arlington, Texas—and dropout of Southern Methodist University—found himself in the shoe business. That year, Blake was traveling in Argentina where he befriended children whom he discovered had no shoes to protect their feet. What he saw sparked an idea and launched a business with a mission that is saving children's lives and turning a profit at the same time. That business is TOMS Shoes.

People laughed when Blake voiced his desire to start a shoe company based on giving away shoes. But despite the objections of others, he began manufacturing lightweight shoes based on the alpargata design that's been worn by Argentine farmers for 100 years. The shoes are made from cotton and canvas, are very comfortable, and now, thanks to TOMS, come in hundreds of styles and fabrics. The soles are constructed of rubber and sometimes made out of rope; some styles even take environmental considerations into account and are vegan as well.

Although Blake's primary motivation was simply to put shoes on children's feet, he concluded—as he was beginning to flesh out his idea—that starting a business rather than a charity would help his impact last longer. Blake's business is totally unique because every time someone buys a pair of TOMS Shoes, another pair is given to a child in need. As with most great and original ideas, he certainly had his detractors in the beginning. Conventional wisdom states that you likely won't stay in business for long using a "One for One" business model. But not only did Blake prove the cynics wrong, by the end of 2009, he estimates that 500,000 pairs of shoes have been given to children since his company's 2006 launch.

All of us are born for a reason, but all of us don't discover why. Success in life has nothing to do with what you gain in life or accomplish for yourself. It's what you do for others.
—Danny Thomas

Blake claims that TOMS Shoes' goal is to not only give shoes, but to also educate people on the importance of this basic article of clothing that so many of us take for granted. For millions of children in developing countries, walking is often the primary mode of transportation. Children frequently have to walk for miles merely to get access to food, water, shelter, and medical help. Wearing shoes allows them to traverse distances that simply aren't possible barefoot. More importantly, wearing shoes prevents children's feet from getting cuts and sores from gravel roads and contaminated soil. These injuries aren't just painful—they're dangerous when they become infected. In fact, the leading cause of disease in developing countries is soil-transmitted parasites that penetrate the skin through open wounds. Simply wearing shoes can prevent this from happening.

"Shoe Drop Tours" are an integral part of TOMS business model; in fact, AT&T filmed one in Uruguay, which they used as a commercial for "staying connected." TOMS schedules shoe drops year-round with help from nonprofit organizations and volunteers. They conduct these drops monthly in Argentina and give away shoes almost every day in Ethiopia. Shoe Drop volunteers are able to hand-deliver shoes to children; and whenever possible, Blake is right there putting shoes on their feet as well.

TOMS received the People's Design Award (a contest sponsored by the Smithsonian's Cooper-Hewitt National Design Museum) in October 2007. In addition, Blake recently attended a meeting with President Obama's administration at the White House with other business leaders to present viable solutions and ideas regarding U.S. economic policy. Blake and TOMS have been featured on numerous television shows, and The Dave Matthews Band sponsored the TOMS vagabond tour to reach campuses nationwide to spread information regarding the One for One movement.

TOMS Shoes is poised to become a model triple bottom line company. Its vision is so inspiring that everyone seems to want to pitch in to help the cause, because TOMS shoes is changing lives while making a sustainable profit.

Never doubt that a small group of committed people can change the world; indeed it is the only thing that ever has.

—Margaret Mead

Step 7:
Dedicate Yourself
to a Lifetime of
Making a
Difference

Orville Wright did not have a pilot's license.

—Gordon McKenzie

No one knows how far the ripple effects of our decisions go, but the decision to give back and make a difference is the highest calling we can aspire to. Successs has little to do with what we accomplish for ourselves, and everything to do with how often we reach out to lighten the burden on others. So how do we walk a mile looking at life through the eyes of the less fortunate? How do we reignite our passion to reach out and help the sick, the suffering, the homeless, and the forgotten?

It is impossible to help someone else without helping yourself in the process.

Mahatma Gandhi was once asked: How do you know if the next act you are about to do is the right one or the wrong one? Gandhi responded by saying, "Consider the face of the poorest most venerable human being that you've ever seen—and ask yourself if the act you contemplate will be of benefit to that person ... If it will, then it's the right thing to do. And if not, then rethink it."

I don't know what your destiny will be, but one thing I do know: the only ones among you who will be really happy are those who have sought and found how to serve.

—Albert Schweitzer

Changing the World Through Service

Service is considered a virtue of every culture in every corner of the globe. It's at the root of almost all religions and belief systems. Countless people have discovered that dedication to a life of service is the path that brings satisfaction and contentment. In the process, people not only change the world, but they change themselves as well.

What Does a Servant-Hearted Person Look Like?

There are myriad stories of people from all walks of life who are quietly changing the world—one act of kindness at a time. There are as many different descriptions of a servant-hearted person as there are humans walking the earth. They are individuals who have made themselves available for others, and for whatever life brings their way. They see the positive side of every situation. They live their lives from an inner conviction that communicates their commitment for reaching out and giving all they can. They might be salt-of-the-earth, simple, caring people who lead unassuming lives but have a fire in their belly that becomes a force to be reckoned with as they reach out to help those less fortunate. Others might be affluent people with above average intelligence who come from a life of privilege and want to use their gifts to help others less fortunate. They make themselves available, because they believe it's their job to do so. They make a concerted effort to change and better others' lives in ways that have an uplifting effect with whomever they come in contact. This in turn attracts others to be with them, work with them, and do business with them.

The Best way to find yourself is to lose yourself in the service of others.

—Mahatma Gandhi

Below are four stories of businesspeople who have found creative ways to reach out and make a difference—people whose efforts are changing the world for the better.

The Songs of Love Foundation

Jeff Jacob, an employee at Crow Company, volunteers his time and songwriting abilities to a unique organization called the Songs of Love Foundation. The outreach was formed 13 years ago by songwriter John Beltzer in an effort to help ease the pain and uncertainty that surrounds terminally and chronically ill children. John began asking fellow songwriters to donate their talents by creating custom songs written specifically for each child.

The organization unites songwriters and recording artists with doctors' offices and hospitals nationwide to harness the healing power of music. To date, nearly 20,000 songs of love have been written, recorded, and distributed as personalized gifts to families and their children. At hundreds of health-care facilities around the world, parents and guardians fill out profile sheets on their ill children, requesting a song of love to be written. These sheets include spaces for children's hobbies, pet names, friends, family names, and other qualities. Songwriters then weave a musical story from those "clues" with the distinct purpose of celebrating each child's unique life in a fun, upbeat fashion.

Approximately 350 songwriters worldwide craft highly personal songs on a tight deadline—and with no budget. Many of these songs are just as much for the family members as they are for the children. Often, the song and CD may become a last memento for family members once a child is gone. The extreme weight of that thought is always on songwriters' minds as they work their craft.

A few years ago, Songs of Love sent Jeff a profile sheet on a child named Jennifer who was battling leukemia. As is often the case, a few weeks after the family had received their song, Jeff received a letter of thanks from Jennifer's mother that said: "Dear Jeff, we play the song you wrote for Jennifer in the car, and in the waiting room every time right before she goes in for chemotherapy. It never fails to make us giggle and feel a bit better, if only for a moment. Thank you for your talent and caring. Sincerely, Abigail. PS: If you're ever in Arkansas, give us a call."

Consider the ripple effect of kindness on all the children who *do* survive their illness—as well as the families of those who don't. Once they are old enough to understand giving, won't they be more apt to run compassionate, innovative companies and organizations? And won't they be more inclined to encourage those around them to do the same?

> *Only a life lived for others is a life worthwhile.*
>   —Albert Einstein

Rocketown

The 1999 high school shooting tragedy at Columbine High School in Colorado seemingly ushered in a new era: one of both violence among our teens, and ultramedia awareness. My friend and client Michael W. Smith was profoundly affected by these events, as he was asked to perform at the memorial service for some of the victims. Michael's experience inspired him to create an outreach organization named Rocketown in downtown Nashville as a haven for inner-city teens who often live in abusive situations and have nowhere to go.

Rocketown houses dance, art, and photography studios, a large music performance venue, a coffee bar, and Tennessee's only indoor skate park. It boasts a well-trained staff of caring, community-minded professionals and volunteers, and offers a vast array of programming— from arts classes to tutoring and mentoring, which are available to all teens. About 1,400 teenagers visit Rocketown each week.

Why is this so important to the local community? Well, Tennessee—and Nashville in particular—have among the worst high school graduation rates in the country for a city of its size. The percentage of those living at or below the poverty line in metro Nashville's public schools is estimated to hover around 70 percent in certain schools. One can therefore assume that most teens don't have many—if any—options to utilize for scholastic help.

I've been on the board of directors for Rocketown for three years, and I can tell you the key to their success is not playing a numbers games for how many children they reach. Rather, it lies in how effectively they can touch the heart and soul of each individual teen. Staff members are dedicated to giving these kids as many options as possible, while teaching them how to form and grow relationships.

Rocketown recently celebrated six years in downtown Nashville, and even with the struggling economy they have helped more teens and their families than ever before. And not only is Rocketown helping thousands of children locally, it has become a resource for other nonprofit and faith-based organizations who are interested in starting similar outreaches in their own communities.

It is one of the most beautiful compensations in life . . . we can never help another without helping ourselves.

—Ralph Waldo Emerson

The Nicaragua Project

Gene Cotton was a hit-singer/songwriter in the 1970s who had ample opportunities to get caught up in the trappings of stardom and the entertainment world. But instead, he decided to use his talents and energy to bend the world into a little bit better place. As the father to three children—two of whom are adopted, including a girl with spinal bifida—Gene is the type of guy who practices what others often preach when it comes to reaching out and helping others.

I remember one Saturday morning 17 years ago, I was working by myself as a carpenter on my first studio when Gene pulled into my drive to say hello. The next thing I knew, he was working alongside me—and continued to do so for the following three days.

Years prior, Gene had begun producing independent films about poor, underserved populations around the world. Doing so drew his attention to poverty-stricken Nicaragua, and prompted him and his wife to visit the war-torn country and become involved with a group called the Nicaragua Project. This organization supports projects such as outfitting dental clinics, providing eye-glasses for the poor, supplying computers to schools, delivering desperately needed supplies to rural medical clinics, improving drinking wells, and providing micro loans for small businesses. Many times Gene has called me to ask if I have any spare, worn-out computers or other supplies that he could take with him on one his trips to this impoverished country.

Why are this organization's actions so important? In addition to the wars and dictators that have wreaked havoc on Nicaragua for decades, Hurricane Mitch in 1998 not only killed thousands of residents, but left the infrastructure and economy devastated as well. As a result of these challenges, this poverty-stricken country boasts a 76 percent unemployment rate, the second highest in the western hemisphere behind only Haiti. Seventy percent of the children who *do* make it to school only reach sixth grade, which begets a tremendous literacy problem.

My purpose here is not simply to sing praises for all this man has done (although he has done a tremendous amount). Rather, I encourage others to see how this single example shines a light on what we can *all* accomplish if we took half the energy and time that Gene has over the years, and devoted those resources to improving the world.

Be the change you want to see in the world.

—Mahatma Gandhi

Feed America First

It was about five years ago that I met Tom Henry for the first time. Sipping on a cup of tea in my office, he described how after 30 years in the restaurant industry he began searching for a higher purpose. Inspired by Bob Buford's book *Halftime,* Tom began evaluating his life in terms of success versus significance, and then began volunteering for Feed the Children in Nashville. That's where Tom began to learn some of the sobering facts about hunger in the United States:

- Forty-nine million Americans must choose between paying for rent, utilities, medicine, or food.
- One in five children (more than 17 million kids) face going to bed or attending school hungry.
- Almost half of the food produced in the United States goes to waste.

It seems that everything in life happens for a reason, and Tom's decades of restaurant experience had equipped him with the perfect skill-sets and experience to embark on a mission to feed the hungry in the United States. He understood that food manufacturers often overproduce to stay ahead of consumer demand, often leaving warehouses overstocked with products they cannot sell, but which they might be willing to donate. Here's the challenge: Tom and his distribution team had to be able to quickly retrieve the food and then have destinations standing by ready to take delivery. It seemed like the perfect vehicle to get food to nearby communities. So Feed America First was born.

Tom began setting up partnerships with scores of small charities in rural areas already engaged in feeding their local communities. Knowing that more food means more lives affected, he simply plugged in by providing this overstocked food to these small outreachers who already knew the needs in their communities.

It is hard to have a bad day when the least you did today was to feed the hungry.

—Tom Henry

Tom left his restaurant business in 2000, and used his severance package to fund his first year. With the help and vision of his partner Don Herbert (who died a year later from kidney cancer), Feed America First started in a pole barn 125 miles from Tom's home. Meanwhile his wife Linda began working a second job to help support the cause.

Fast-forward to the present: Tom still keeps finances close to the vest in order to be as effective as possible. The entire operation is staffed with only three people along with the help of volunteers, yet in 2008 Feed America First distributed 3.5 million pounds of food, all while using only $172,000 in expenses . . . about a nickel a pound. In fact, Feed America First has been able to provide enough food for 13 meals for each dollar donated, all while maintaining an overhead of 4 percent to 6 percent. Now that's efficiency!

In the near future Tom envisions franchising his model out to help others establish a similar operation in their areas. I am so excited about the potential of Feed America First, I recorded and released a new CD, *The Seventh Step,* in which 100 percent of the gross income will go to this organization.

Not only is Tom helping to give thousands of people a hand up, but in doing so he's also increasing the odds that those millions of hungry citizens will be able to add their contributions to our workforce and make the United States stronger. Feed America First is a shining example of how everyone can make a measurable difference in the world.

> *The miracle is this—the more we share, the more we have.*
>
> —Leonard Nimoy

What Can You Do to Make a Difference?

Although it's easy to succumb to pessimistic thoughts of fear, frustration, and scarcity, people who reach out and give of themselves tend to attract abundance into their lives in unimaginable ways. The same can be true for your business. Creating ways for your company to reach beyond the bottom line by partnering with and supporting worthy philanthropic endeavors will bring a renewed sense of purpose for your employees and partners. That outreach will energize everyone in your business to be more energetic and enthusiastic at work each day.

It's time to ask yourself: "What can I do to make a difference?" Although you might not see someone who can change the world when you look in the mirror, a homeless man or woman may see you as a caring friend who can give them a hand. An abused child from a broken home might see a mentor in you. A senior citizen with no family might see you as a lifeline. These people don't care about your career title or financial status. To them, you're simply someone who cares and can make a difference in their lives.

True success has little to do with what we accomplish for ourselves, and everything to do with how we reach out to others. If we all give according to our abilities, the positive impact will be staggering—because each of us can use our unique gifts to lift spirits, touch hearts, and become powerful agents of change in the world.

> These are the times that try men's souls; but giving back and making a difference just might be the medicine that will turn our world around.

30-Day Pledge

In the next 30 days I _____
[insert name] make the following commitments to improve my personal life, professional life, and the lives of those in the greater world community by taking the steps that follow. I will use the outline as a resource to make every effort to become a leader who will make a difference.

Name: _____

Date: _____

Signature: _____

I pledge to . . . *exceed expectations* in the lives I touch at work and at home.

By taking these steps: _____

_____

_____

_____

I pledge to . . . make daily *measurable improvement* in my business.

By taking these steps: _____

_____

_____

_____

I pledge to . . . develop an *accountability matrix* for my business
   and life.
By taking these steps: _____

_____

_____

_____

I pledge to . . . reinvigorate my business through *multidimensional thinking.*
By taking these steps: _____

_____

_____

_____

I pledge to . . . develop a culture of *shared sacrifice.*
By taking these steps: _____

_____

_____

_____

I pledge to . . . develop a *triple bottom line* business philosophy.
By taking these steps: _____

_____

_____

_____

I pledge to . . . dedicate myself to a lifetime of *making a
   difference.*
By taking these steps: _____

_____

_____

_____

Now Is the Time

It's not what you are that holds you back, it's what you think you are not.

—Denis Waitley

Evolving is a choice.

It's your choice to embrace change.

Your future successes will be in direct proportion to your ability to adapt to those changes.

Never before in the history of humankind have we been so overwhelmed with the magnitude and complexity of issues that we currently face. Though these are troubling times, it is times such as these that force us to try harder, dig deeper, and discover strengths we never knew we had. Whether your company has been around for decades, or you're a young entrepreneur starting a business—you are up against some enormous challenges. But with adversity comes opportunity. You have within your grasp the capability and the resources fueled by the unbreakable human spirit to not only meet these challenges, but to create sustainable, profitable business solutions that will make the world a better place in the process.

Now is the time . . .

Now is the time to *choose* innovation over statuesque.

Now is the time to *choose* responsibility over blame.

Now is the time to *choose* efficiency over expediency.

Now is the time to *choose* long-term vision over short-term gain.

Now is the time to *choose* to be a leader who will make a difference.

Resources

Books

Bossidy, Larry, and Ram Charan. *Execution: The Discipline of Getting Things Done*. New York: Crown Publishing Group, 2002.

Branson, Richard. *Business Stripped Bare: Adventures of a Global Entrepreneur*. London: Virgin Books, 2008.

Braungart, Michael, and William McDonough. *Cradle to Cradle: Remaking the Way We Make Things*. New York: North Point Press, 2002.

Calloway, Joe. *Indispensable: How to Become the Company That Your Customers Can't Live Without*. Hoboken, NJ: John Wiley & Sons, 2005.

Clinton, Bill. *Giving: How Each of Us Can Change the World*. New York: Alfred A. Knopf, 2007.

Collins, Jim. *Good to Great: Why Some Companies Make the Leap . . . and Others Don't*. New York: HarperCollins, 2001.

Dent, Harry S., Jr. *The Roaring 2000s: Building the Wealth and Lifestyle You Desire in the Greatest Boom in History*. New York: Simon & Schuster, 1998.

Diamond, Jared. *Collapse: How Societies Choose to Fail or Succeed*. New York: Penguin Group, 2005.

Flannery, Tim. *The Weather Makers: How Man Is Changing the Climate and What It Means for Life on Earth*. Melbourne, Australia: Text Publishing Company, 2005.

Gladwell, Malcolm. *Outliers: The Story of Success*. New York: Little, Brown, 2008.

Glennon, Robert. *Unquenchable: America's Water Crisis and What to Do about It*. Washington, DC: Island Press, 2009.

Goodell, Jeff. *Big Coal: The Dirty Secret Behind America's Energy Future.* Boston: Houghton Mifflin, 2007.

Gore, Al. *An Inconvenient Truth: The Planetary Emergency of Global Warming and What We Can Do about It.* Emmaus, PA: Rodale, 2006.

Gore, Al. *Our Choice: A Plan to Solve the Climate Crisis.* New York: Simon & Schuster, 2009.

Heinberg, Richard. *Blackout: Coal, Climate and the Last Energy Crisis.* Gabriola, BC: New Society Publishers, 2009.

Heinberg, Richard. *The Party's Over: Oil, Water and the Fate of Industrial Societies.* Gabriola, BC: New Society Publishers, 2003.

Heinberg, Richard. *Peak Everything: Waking Up to the Century of Decline.* Gabriola, BC: New Society Publishers, 2007.

Heinberg, Richard. *Power Down: Options and Actions for a Post-Carbon World.* Gabriola, BC: New Society Publishers, 2004.

Hirshberg, Gary. *Stirring It Up: How to Make Money and Save the World.* New York: Hyperion, 2008.

Iacocca, Lee, and Catherine Whitney. *Where Have All the Leaders Gone?* New York: Simon & Schuster, 2007.

Lynas, Mark. *Six Degrees: Our Future on a Hotter Planet.* Washington, DC: National Geographic Society, 2008.

Meadows, Dennis L., Donella H. Meadows, and Jørgen Randers. *Beyond the Limits: Confronting Global Collapse, Envisioning a Sustainable Future.* White River Junction, VT: Chelsea Green Publishing Company, 1992.

Michelli, Joseph, A. *The Starbucks Experience: 5 Principles for Turning Ordinary into Extraordinary.* New York: McGraw-Hill, 2007.

Obama, Barack. *The Audacity of Hope: Thoughts on Reclaiming the American Dream.* New York: Crown Publishers, 2006.

Pearce, Fred. *Confessions of an Eco-Sinner: Tracking Down the Sources of My Stuff.* Boston: Beacon Press, 2008.

Pearce, Fred. *With Speed and Violence: Why Scientists Fear Tipping Points in Climate Change.* Boston: Beacon Press, 2007.

Pelletier, Ray. *It's All about Service: How to Lead Your People to Care for Your Customers.* Hoboken, NJ: John Wiley & Sons, 2005.

Pickens, T. Boone. *The First Billion Is the Hardest.* New York: Crown Business, 2008.

Poscente, Vince. *The Age of Speed: Learning to Thrive in a More-Faster-Now World*. Austin, TX: Bard Press, 2008.

Quinn, Robert E. *Building the Bridge as You Walk on It: A Guide for Leading Change*. San Francisco: Jossey-Bass, 2004.

Richardson, Bill. *Leading by Example: How We Can Inspire an Energy and Security Revolution*. Hoboken, NJ: John Wiley & Sons, 2008.

Schor, Juliet B. *The Overspent American: Upscaling, Downshifting, and the New Consumer*. New York: Basic Books, 1998.

Spence, Chris. *Global Warming: Personal Solutions for a Healthy Planet*. New York: Palgrave Macmillan, 2005.

Steiner, Christopher. *$20 Per Gallon: How the Inevitable Rise in the Price of Gasoline Will Change Our Lives for the Better*. New York: Grand Central Publishing, 2009.

Surviving Change: A Manager's Guide. Boston: Harvard Business School Press, 2009.

Welch, Jack, with John A. Byrne. *Jack: Straight from the Gut*. New York: Warner Business Books, 2001.

Welch, Jack, and Suzy Welch. *Winning*. New York: HarperCollins Publishers, 2005.

DVDs

The 11th Hour. Prod. Leonardo DiCaprio. Warner Independent Pictures, 2007.

Flow: How Did a Handful of Corporations Steal Our Water? Oscilloscope Pictures, 2008.

Global Warming: The Signs and the Science. Prod. Stonehaven Production Services and South Carolina ETV. PBS Video, 2005.

Global Warming: What's Up with the Weather? Dir. Jon Palfreman. A Frontline/NOVA co-production with the Palfreman Film Group, 2000.

Green: The New Red, White and Blue. Discovery Channel, 2007.

An Inconvenient Truth. Perf. Al Gore. Dir. Davis Guggenheim. Lawrence Bender Productions, 2006.

Kilowatt Ours: A Plan to Re-Energize America. Dir. Jeff Barrie. National
  Edition, 2007.
Last Days on Earth. ABC News Inc. and A&E Television Networks. The
  History Channel, 2006.
Sicko. Dir. Michael Moore. Weinstein Company, 2007.
Too Hot Not to Handle. Prod. Laurie David. HBO Documentary Films, 2006.
Who Killed the Electric Car? Dir. Chris Pane. Sony Pictures, 2006.

Web Sites

Chris Martenson: www.chrismartenson.com
Climate Change: www.climatechange.com
Climate Crisis: www.climatecrisis.net
The Coming Global Oil Crisis: www.oilcrisis.com
Current News: http://current.com
Darkhorse Recording Studio: www.darkhorse.com
Environmental News Service: www.mywire.com
Natural Resources Defense Council: www.nrdc.org
Robin Crow: www.robincrow.com
Solar Energy International: www.solarenergy.org
Tree Media Group: www.treemedia.com
World Watch Institute: www.worldwatch.org